ADVANCE PRAISE

Journeys get easier when the map is good. The seven-step plan in Masterstrokes is just the roadmap you need to navigate the future in your own leadership journey. Don't leave home without it!

Prakash Iyer, *Leadership Coach and Motivational Speaker*

Leadership is a journey, one where different leaders end in different destinations—true leadership is exhibited more in the journey, showing the Being of the leader.

This book brings into exploration of the Being of the leader— awareness, action, facing uncertainty, reflection, ownership and, more importantly, purpose. Dr Latha easily transcends the various components of leadership, as if she is a commentator in the journey like a Sanjaya in Mahabharat. This will be a landmark book on leadership—one that I will read multiple times.

R. K. T. Krishnan, *Country Head, Corporate Sales at Royal Sundaram General Insurance Co.*

The book is a masterstroke! It brings alive the nuanced stance of a Coach triggering thought-provoking inquiry to the norms, roles, context of leadership as we knew it.

A very relevant book given the current reality of the VUCA world where leaders travel uncharted paths with no known norms, formats, dictats to fall back on. It's a call for a clear shift in re-imagining a Leader's journey. The author's grasp of the current context and the conversational style laced with humour drawing from ancient folklore and mythology makes this a delightful read.

Priya Ramesh, *Leadership Coach Co-Founder, Orenda Centre for Leadership Excellence*

There is a need for leaders to learn and re-learn often on Leadership for uncertain times. This book attempts to provide a great learning to all on leading in uncertain times. The approach of the book on defining a problem, taking through a journey and building a leader is incredible, which gives greater insights to the readers. I am sure this book will help young managers and leaders to script their own personal leadership narrative and build passion within to reach success.

Dr Anbuthambi Bhojarajan, *President, ICT Academy*

Masterstokes: Reinventing Leadership in Uncertain Times is a timely and contextual book set in current times. It is enlightening and moving, centred around a dialogue between a Leader and his Coach. It has many practical and actionable lessons for everyone. It is a welcome addition to the leadership book bag.

Sridhar Ganesh, *Managing Director & CEO, Adrenalin eSystems Limited*

Dr Latha's latest work, comes at a timely juncture, reminding leaders—new and existing—that leadership is a journey and a narrative that needs to involve and engage all. 'We must change the way we do business in this world of permanent excess supply,' a quote from the book that is a fitting reminder of how the world has changed and that no individual leader can be a superhero to thrive in the longer run. Dr Latha cleverly weaves in stories whilst unfolding the leadership narrative through her seven-step model (STROKES) that can help you rewrite your leadership story.

Janet Yung, *Chief Learning Officer & Director, Trilogy People Performance Consultancy*

Intensifying global competition, rising performance expectations and proliferating social and economic problems everywhere have put an unprecedented premium on leadership. This book will describe the areas you need to excel and how to build those abilities. Dr Latha Vijaybaskar provides ambitious professionals with the frameworks, guidance and tools they need to excel in their careers. With step-by-step framework, time-honed best practices, real-life stories and concise models, each comprehensive chapter will help you to stand out from the pack—whatever your role.

Alison Geskin, *ACC CODC CEC CLC Founder*
and CEO, The Art of Strategy

Dr Latha in her book takes us through an awesome journey of leadership through the perspectives of Arjun and Ved. It's refreshing to see the new thought process that is essential for leaders in these changing times. I especially loved the book's narrative style that kept me engaged throughout reading. If you care deeply about building leadership qualities and if you want to pick up subtle nuances, put this book on your essential reading list.

Sivakumar Palaniappan,
Leadership Mindset Coach

Know the different hues of leadership which help to take on any unforeseen challenges. The story line is engaging and adds a good flavour to the aspects of what it takes to be a good leader.

Sangeeta Shankaran Sumesh, *The Gain Enabler*
High Performance Business Coach & Best Selling Author

A very conversational and relatable way of storytelling with the required intersections of making the reader correlate story to reality and back to the story. The pauses make the impact that much more appealing and stick to memory. Characters are built around concepts and then new concepts are introduced to ensure that characters go through the growth curve in their minds. Appreciate the thought that went into sketching and then stitching it all together seamlessly. Will endorse the book and encourage young and matured managers alike to give the book a *dekho*!

Kanishka Mallick, *General Manager, HR Times Internet*

Master Strokes

reinventing leadership in uncertain times

Latha Vijaybaskar

 SAGE |
Response
Business Books

Los Angeles | London | New Delhi
Singapore | Washington DC | Melbourne

First published in 2021 by

SAGE Publications India Pvt. Ltd
B1/I-1 Mohan Cooperative Industrial Area
Mathura Road, New Delhi 110 044, India
www.sagepub.in

SAGE Publications Inc
2455 Teller Road
Thousand Oaks, California 91320, USA

SAGE Publications Ltd
1 Oliver's Yard, 55 City Road
London EC1Y 1SP, United Kingdom

SAGE Publications Asia-Pacific Pte Ltd
18 Cross Street #10-10/11/12
China Square Central
Singapore 048423

Published by Vivek Mehra for SAGE Publications India Pvt. Ltd. Typeset in 9.5/13.5 pt ITC Stone Serif and Rockwell, 9/13 pt, by Fidus Design Pvt. Ltd, Chandigarh.

Library of Congress Cataloging-in-Publication Data Available

ISBN: 978-93-5388-706-3 (PB)

SAGE Team: Neha Pal, Ankit Verma, Megha Dabral and Rajinder Kaur
Illustration credit: Shriram Vijaybaskar

To
Priyanka and Shriram.
Always.

CONTENTS

It gives me great pleasure to write a foreword to this insightful book authored by Latha. I have known her to be an astute behavioural scientist with a keen eye on leadership matters.

Leadership is one of the complex paradigms whose complete understanding continues to elude the pundits. No wonder then that we have zillions of books, publications, action research, development programs and evaluations on this topic.

Through her lucid yet insightful expression, Latha has sewn many gems into the tales that she has woven together as a beautiful fabric. The complex and myriad aspects of leadership have been dealt with in a manner that awakens the reader with subtle nudges.

Provoking us into pondering over the very definition of a leader– in the context that we live in today,– Latha reveals the reality to us. She has used the rich repository of Indian wisdom, drawing lessons and parallels from the epics like the Mahabharata and other interesting stories from the *Vetaalapanchashati*.

'Masterstrokes...' interestingly enmeshes the modern psychological constructs with the interpretations of ancient Indian wisdom with leadership in corporate settings. The play of shadows, the ARC (read the book to know more) and the seven stages of becoming a good leader are interesting chapters.

Not only does Latha analyse leadership and its complexity, she also provides the reader with a step-by-step approach to becoming a good leader. Like ARC, she also uses easy-to-remember tricks like V.I.T.A.L and provides a toolkit to help the reader self-assess and become more self-aware.

Like her first book on having difficult conversations, many readers will benefit from this work. Wish you all a happy reading.

Arvind Subramanian
Vice President, Human Resources at
Reliance Industries Limited

Dear Leader,

I am immensely grateful that you have this book in your hands right now. My deep hope is that for you as a leader positioned on the edge of the dividing line from known stories to unchartered waters, this book serves as a guide that effect heroic transformations in your leadership narrative.

Masterstrokes is based on the concept that leadership is a journey, one that carries the experiences of the past but looks towards the future. I began this book as an extension to my research on millennial leadership and my ongoing quest to 'rewrite your story, reclaim your life'.

The book explores leadership essentially as a humanistic approach with leaders understanding their self and shadows, developing a holistic mindset and rewriting their narratives in this multidimensional, multilevel journey.

The book is a dialogue, a conversation between a mentor and a CEO. The uniqueness of the dialogue lies in the numerous stories that the mentor shares to lead towards a leadership concept. In this regard, stories form the content and context of the book.

Some of the unique features that you as a leader will explore in the book are how a leader is part of the problem? How to identify shadows and the dark side of leadership? How can you as a leader develop a mindset of adaptive resilience? How can a leader lead in times of uncertainty with changing followership, business ecosystems and ways of working?

I hope you as a leader find the lessons to lead yourself and your team.

Love and respect,
Dr Latha Vijaybaskar

ACKNOWLEDGEMENTS

Masterstrokes is a journey, and many have travelled this path with me. This book, right from its inception, has been a collective query of many, and a part of my ongoing quest to rewrite a life of your dreams. I am grateful to my clients, students and participants in my workshops for bringing this book to life. If not for you, these conversations would have been wrapped up at the end of a coaching session.

From thoughts to words was difficult but the journey from a draft to a published copy is a writer's nightmare. Special thanks to Neha Pal, of SAGE, and her team who has lovingly crafted every sentence of this book with me. Thank you, team; you made this journey a lot less arduous than it would have been and thanks for putting up with me patiently when I missed yet another deadline. Special thanks to all my initial readers who have read and endorsed my efforts. My deepest gratitude to Aravind Subramanian who chaired the session where I first presented a part of my research and has supported me with his insight as a seasoned HR practitioner as well as penned the foreword to the book.

My muse to writing a good copy have been my husband and two kids, Priyanka and Shriram, who have pushed me to achieve all that I dreamt of. They have played the tough dual role of being my fan and severe critic, balancing the insanity with grace and wit.

And now, thank you, reader! By reading this book and every time you brave yourself to lead into the future, you make my vision come true.

PART 1

The Problem

1 THE CRASHING WORLD OF ARJUN RAGHAVAN

If you remain silent, you die; if you speak, you lose.

Arjun smiled for the first time that day as he turned into the parking of the office of the Corporate *Vetaal*. The front had an upside-down vampire hanging from a tree with a welcome signboard that read, 'If you remain silent, you die; if you speak, you lose.'

This place has all the looks of his irreverent friend Ved—who is nowadays called the corporate Vetaal. If anyone could help him out of the mess he has dug himself into, it would be Ved. Arjun quickly parked his car and moved towards the grinning vampire.

Arjun and Ved were schoolmates and great friends in their childhood. Passage of time, parents' work needs and their different career paths managed to keep them on different tracks in life. They lost touch until recently when Arjun read about the corporate Vetaal in a magazine. He had quickly reached out to Ved and here he was, with the corporate Vetaal who greeted him in a black T-shirt, jeans and a bandana on his head—laugh lines liberal on the curve of his mouth and eyes.

'Ved, you are just what I need right now', Arjun said with a tight hug that had Ved laughing.

'My world is collapsing and I don't know how to fight it.'

Ved smiled his welcome, 'Come on in and let us hear all about your crashing world'.

Arjun walked into a room that looked like a themed cafe. Something like Goth meets Boho with shades of both fairy tales and horror elements. Curious of the décor yet too troubled to question, Arjun was silent while they sat down on chairs with a claw-shaped wooden table between them.

'Tell me more', Ved invited.

Arjun fell silent, sunk in thought. Ved allowed this silence to comfort him. Finally, Arjun began, 'We are now a 100 crore company. We have 150 people on the team now and business is on a growth spurt.'

'When I started out, it was a heady need to challenge the existing limitations of the international bank I worked for and provide the customers what my celebrated bank could not. In fact, a particular case of a woman in absolute need of a loan that I could not pass through—due to rules—firmed my decision.'

'In 2012, I moved out and started "MOOLA" a 100 per cent online marketplace for peer-to-peer lending. My burning need to remove the friction in the borrowing places made me create a platform like Ola and Uber but for peer-to-peer borrowing and lending.'

'The last eight years have seen steady growth for the company. As we were not funded, from inception we are cockroaches. Strategize, plan, cut costs, stretch, execute has been our mantra, and my initial team believed this, so we forged ahead with a solid focus.'

'In three years' time, Moola grew to be a 25-member team and slowly we moved to create a more concrete organization structures. Aparna joined us to head HR. She had three years' experience in a large IT company and we brought her in, as she is one energetic and people-oriented person. She is a true nurturer and has a compassionate ear to all.'

'In the coming years, our 25-member team kept growing due to some heroic efforts in customer experience and innovative partnership ideas. Each year's success built as a stepping-stone to our success foundation.'

'And that's when things really changed. The last couple of years have been hectic. We kept adding new members and are now at 150 people. Raj joined us four years back to head sales. He is a friend from my old company, and he came in at a time when I was looking for someone who could aggressively control the channel. Raj is hard-working and a no-nonsense person. But in the last one year, the sales team faced a huge increase in performance-related attrition. In fact, some of our better sales guys have quit. The most perplexing fact is, a few of these people had no other job offer, are not the rich kids in the neighbourhood and yet they did not grab our increment offer. We introduced a new incentive scheme that was biting into our profits and we thought the sales team will be overjoyed, but they did not bite that bullet. Raj is cracking his brains on what will make them work hard and what will make them stay.'

'We also had a stray case in integrity. As a lending organization, we are prepared for the lenders to default. That is part of how the business works. But one of our sales guys created fake lenders, made them borrow money, he got a share of the loot and then asked the lender to default.'

'The problem is, Ved, I don't even know many of these boys now. When we started out, the team was small and we lived like a family. Holed up first in my apartment then in a rented place with zero facilities, the bunch of us were extremely fired up to succeed. Today the team is huge, we have various reporting systems and more than 75 per cent of the team is filled with the younger generation. And they, believe me, are a different nut to crack.'

'The numbers in our balance sheet, both actuals and our forecast tell only a fraction of the story. Our survival is not primarily in the numbers, it's not in our technological leadership, it's not in our long-standing 'Moola' brand name, it's not in another cost-saving round and more strategic partnerships.'

'Our success today depends on creating partnerships with more of the emerging generation, creating confidence in the minds of our stakeholders, creating a sense of pride among our team and most importantly understanding what motivates everyone and how they can achieve their dreams through us.'

'But so far, we have mostly only managed numbers, selected facts and technical questions and selected data. We have to do a lot better if we want to keep this company in business.'

'When the company was small, we had a more personalized approach to the whole borrowing and lending process. We had this strong relationship with all our lenders, we made them feel privileged and the borrowers were empowered. Priya and Mahesh lead the partnerships. They worked with each stakeholder meticulously and every partnership was celebrated like a life saved. Now we have so many on board, the partnerships are a name on the excel sheet and Priya and Mahesh no more have any personal contact with the partners. They have set up some great systems but the team misses on the fun. It has become a routine work nowadays. This makes it difficult to drum up interest and passion in the team. As the entire idea of the business is to democratize borrowing and lending, it is important for every member in my team to believe every touchpoint in and out of the company is king. Or else the personal relationship would be lost and we will be working like robots. That cannot happen as our operations work predominantly on trust. The lender needs to trust us; the borrower needs to trust us. Every team member needs to believe in this and work with passion. I feel that element missing. When we were 25, I could confidently say, our culture was built on our passion and hard work. Now that is diluted and distracted and our core team just does not know how to deal with this.'

'At the heart of all this is the technical team. In the beginning, this was the most important team in our organization as we had everything online and needed the best that technology could provide. We have a great system now and a team to oversee any glitches. Vignesh, who has been with me from inception, was the mastermind behind everything related to technology at Moola. Today he is on the verge of giving up because his team is made of two sets of people, a division that the organization structure did not create. One set calls themselves the 'nuts' and are forever coming to Vignesh with ideas in AI or new bots or any new technology that's out there. This group gets angry when their ideas are shot down mostly because such an expense is not budgeted and approved. The group also comes in and goes at all times and this angers the other divided groups who are nicknamed bolts by the nuts. The bolts manage the regular day-to-day work of managing a completely online company running smoothly. But this is a mundane work. The motivation to do the maintenance work is on a downward spiral among this group. Also, this group works in shifts and therefore has specific work timings, a sore point of the team with the 'come and go as I please' nuts group. Vignesh says he feels like a clown in a circus, trying to keep a smiling face amidst crumbling blocks.'

'The responsibility to lead under these circumstances is not a privilege. It is a heavy burden, demanding humility and sacrifices. Sometimes I feel leading this team now is a trip down a rabbit hole.'

'Ved, my revenue today has not shown too many changes but I worry that will change. We have grown in numbers and maybe I am not sure how to lead them. I am also worried that my second line of defence is not geared up to lead. Priya, Vignesh, Mahesh and Aparna are my pillars and we, as a whole, need to lead better. If I were to summarize my needs, I would say, I want

- To understand my changing followers. This new bunch has so much potential and I want to know how to leverage.

- To know how to stay ahead of the market. We have enough issues with government rules changing overnight, RBI and the mercurial market. How do I stay on top of this game?

- To blend both my team and the chaos around in such a way that we still move ahead in our goals steadily.'

Ved listened the entire time attentively with a soft smile that was both compassionate and encouraging. 'Arjun, if you were to frame what you want in a sentence, what would that be?'

'I am looking for a business and leadership masterstroke—one that would take me, and my team, towards lasting success.'

He now asked a simple question, 'What does leadership mean to you?'

Arjun was a bit confused, 'Is that an academic question?'

'No, it is a very personal question and I want you to give your answer and not a quote or definition. Try another angle—Who, according to you is a good leader and who is a bad leader?'

Arjun smiled. 'A good leader is one who has figured out how to solve all the problems, creates processes and puts systems in place for the smooth functioning of the organization and inspires his people to succeed. A bad leader is probably someone who has not figured out these things.'

Ved asked with his eyes twinkling, 'So are you a good leader or bad?'

Arjun was lost. 'I try to solve the problems Ved, but they keep piling. So, am I a bad leader?

Or am I looking at leadership through the wrong lens?'

ARJUN'S NOTES: MY LEADERSHIP MASTERSTROKE

1. What does leadership mean to me?
2. Is leadership a role? A process? A responsibility? an Ability?
3. Who is a good leader? Who is a bad leader?

 # THE NEED FOR A NEW LEADERSHIP NARRATIVE

Ved smiled as Arjun processed the good leader question.

'Arjun, do you know why I call myself the corporate Vetaal?' Ved asked.

'Oh, I think it's great marketing, you with the unique look calling yourself a vampire. A style statement, one I am sure works great with the current game addicted generation', Arjun replied

'Not at all. It has a personal and passionate reason. As a child, I have always been fascinated with stories. We all live by stories. Stories convert the mere data we have to an emotional thread from start to finish. A thousand people dead in an earthquake is data, it does not induce much of emotion. But a movie based on the incident that shows the protagonist trying hard to save the people, now that brings out all our emotions. Stories are powerful. Leadership is, in essence, a humanistic pursuit and can be better understood with stories than strategies.

'And of all the stories, the quirky paradox of the vampire storyteller Vetaal, much like our work lives, is a realm of the most intricate and brilliant storytelling ever woven. It is a frame narrative, stories nested within stories, and forms the largest single collection known to man. The *kathasarisagar* [1], the ocean of stories written by *Somadeva* in the 11th century that forms the inspiration to the Arabian tales is a seat of all answers and my favourite bedtime story as a child.

'Inside this oceanic labyrinth lies the *Vetaala Panchavimshati* that was translated in the 19th century to *Betaal Pachisi*—25 tales of Betaal.'

The noble hero of the *Vetaala Panchavimshati* is the legendary king *Vikramaditya* of Ujjain. An ascetic comes to meet the king one fine day gifting him with fruits. One of the fruits falls and a ruby is revealed inside. Now the curious king and his men cut open all the fruits and as, magical tales would have it, there lies a ruby in every one of the fruits. Of course, Vikram wants to know more. The ascetic who is actually a *vamachari* (sorcerer) asks Vikram of a heroic act to complete his rituals. Vikram has to fetch him the Vetaal—the ghoul vampire that hangs upside down from the tree in the crematorium.

Faithful to his promise, the determined king Vikram sets out towards his task, the warning to not talk to the Vetaal ringing in his ears.

He finds Vetaal upside down and tries to carry him. The vampire slips away. After a few tries, he manages to carry Vetaal on his back. The Vetaal is a consummate storyteller and offers to tell a story to pass time. His stories end with questions that are witty, rich in philosophical thinking and based on the socio-cultural settings of those times. Of course, there is a paradox—if the king knows the answer and does not answer, his head will burst into a hundred pieces. If he opens his mouth to answer, the Vetaal will fly back to the tree.

And, thus, begins a series of stories, 24 to be exact where Vetaal the narrator is neither alive nor dead, Vikram as a listener can neither speak nor remain silent, the questions posed are subjective, dissolving the lines between right and wrong, duty and desire, life and death.

'To me, this Vampire is much like a coach, a narrative method to show the problem and powerful questions that help you think. I use the same method and help people look into their problems in a way their spreadsheets and balance sheets don't. I help them look into their stories, and as a coach, ask powerful questions to empower them towards their solutions. So, my being the corporate Vetaal is helping others see through the lens of Vetaal, a wise narrative coach.'

'Anyway, back to the story,' on the 25th attempt, the Vetaal tells the story of a father and a son in the aftermath of a devastating war. In the woods, they see human footprints and assume they belong to women. The king and the prince agree that if they were to meet the women, the father would marry the woman with the larger feet and the son would marry the woman with the smaller feet. They do meet the women in the forest, but the larger feet belong to the daughter and the smaller feet to her mother. As per their agreement, the king marries the daughter and his son marries her mother. Eventually, the son and the queen and the father and the princess have children.

'The Vetaal asks, 'Tell me, Oh King, what's the relation between the two new-born children is?' The question stumps Vikram. Creating a family tree in this situation is a catastrophe to civilizational meanings.

In the ensuing silence and the closure of the cycle of tales, Vikramaditya successfully carries Vetaal to the sorcerer.

WHERE MEANINGS END, THE STORIES END...THEIR ATTACHED PHILOSOPHIES AND THEORIES END

'Now I ask you—Have we come to the last tale in leadership? Are we standing in a time where what stories we have heard and learnt can no longer help us? Do we need to look at leadership through a new lens?'

Like King Vikram, Arjun also did not have an answer.

'Remember tales end when the society no longer understands the context and meaning in them. Leadership, as we know it, has come to an end. It is time we change our narratives, our success tales, and weave a different story.'

'Let's consider the modern workplace today and I will leave you to draw the parallels.'

'From the times of the king to the modern theorists, in leadership everyone follows the leadership tripod rule. The theories of leadership focus on a linear process of developing the "leader" so that the "follower" listens and follows to achieve the "goal". This very much looks like paddling in a river. The rowers listen to a leader, follow their process of rowing the boat with the firm belief that it will take them to the shore.'

'But this is a past story. Today the calm river is white water. Swirling change, turbulent flow and rocky paths are the norms. The first leg, the 'goal' which is the strategic and operating landscape of a business in the current VUCA age is constantly unsettled. The uncertainty and complexity coupled with speed and dynamics of change have made these goals unrecognizable and unpredictable. So, leadership for a particular goal makes the process unprepared for uncertain susceptibilities and vulnerabilities.'

'So how do you contribute effectively to making a positive difference amidst the complexity and uncertainty? '

'The traditional stories will have a superhero to help us out of this swirling river—a great leader who will help us sail through the churning waters like the unrealistic movies. While the pull of the hero is attractive, it is an escapist fantasy. The allure is both naive and dangerous. The superhero leader can go two ways:

1. The leader feels he is an all-powerful and the inter-galactic king. This may lead to imposing edicts and rules and creating a kind of monopoly that history has often seen end in tragic collapse. In such places, the morale decreases; productivity takes a nosedive; trust, vision, and accountability become mere words and the only thing on an upward curve is the attrition rate.

2. A more realistic picture being today leadership is multidimensional and overwhelms an individual leader's cognitive abilities. Because no individual is likely to embody all the traits, the idea of a single hero leading the ship to success through turbulent waters is difficult.

Can one leader do it all? If the leader cannot lead, whom do we follow? How do we get things done? It is after all uncertain times!

Ah, the classic follower—the abiding, loyal employee whose mention brings in happy memories of simpler times.

Where is he?'

'The current workplace has a reigning majority of millennials—a generation that is redefining organizational hierarchies. The traditional heroic top-down image of a leader in the driver's seat and followers as passive travellers does not work with the millennial. They are also confident of their good work and demand respect. Meanwhile, the factor of 'tyranny' consists of variables such as domineering, pushy, controlling and coercive, which is in contradiction with the millennials' characters.'

'Therefore, like the last tale of Vikram and Vetaal, we are now at the end of our leadership tale and, for the newer and emerging business landscape, need to write new stories.'

Arjun now jumps in, 'I volunteer. First tale. as a business expands, more people come in; the culture and role of a leader drastically change. The team play their own game and the rules change. New government rules, changes in the economy and turbulent lender and borrower dynamics give this tale more action. So yes, we change the tale. How can leaders behave differently and do things better?'

Ved says, 'Let Vetaal tell us another story!'

'This time around let's start with the climax...after all, we by now know that listening to a Vetaal tale is a build-up towards the question.'

In the story, we have a very beautiful woman Sundari—I leave it to your imagination to define beauty. We have a loyal brother and a loving husband. By divine caprice, Sundari finds them dead. Beheaded. Just as she is about to kill herself, Sundari suddenly faces the Goddess who grants the wish for the bodies to become alive. An overjoyed Sundari quickly arranges the head and body and by the divine powers, the men are alive. Just that the body of the brother is matched to head of the husband and the head of the brother to the body of the husband.

'Vetaal's question, of course, is now who is the husband and who is the brother?'

'Vetaal's question of mixing heads and bodies is common to us in many of the promotion stories in our organizations. The person who does a great job is promoted to manage others to do a great job.

Arjun, tell me what is your actual role in your organization today? Is it managing your 150 people or even the four pillars you have?' Ved suddenly stopped his stories to ask yet another question.

Arjun was silent for a while. He then replied contemplating the previous questions and adding this new one, 'Ved, while I understand that theoretically the books and speeches say that a job of a leader is to create more leaders, to transform the culture and such things, but the hard fact is when 9 am hits, everyone just gets down to business and managing to create transformation as part of mundane life is something that I don't have a clue about.'

Ved thought for a while. 'Hmm, I agree.'

Leadership is generally easy—until you hit a wall. When that happens, leadership is a lonely job of clearing up the mess and creating new ones in its place.

'The danger lines flash when using the word "leader" to describe someone as it confuses concepts of exercising leadership with notions of positional authority.

'What does this look like in practice?

'Imagine you are in a two-storied building. The building is on fire and you have run up to the terrace. You know the only way now is to jump. You will get hurt but will be alive. What do you do?'

Arjun replied immediately—'jump'.

'Exactly. Now imagine you are on that terrace and slowly all your employees also land up there. What will you do?

'Would you ask them all to jump?

'And more importantly, will they jump if you ask?'

Arjun answered slowly, 'I guess it is prudent to ask them to jump. But I am not sure. There will be a mess, people will fall and can be killed in the stampede. Everyone can jump together and there may be a pile of fallen bodies on the ground. A few may not listen to me and try something else. With the bunch of youngsters I have, maybe they will experiment becoming superheroes.

'I am reminded of that story of the boy whose music made the rats and later all the kids follow him, Pied Piper. Well, if I were Pied

Piper, then maybe all will jump the way I want them to—or if we all had some military training.'

Ved replied, 'The problem is not that we are not Pied Pipers, but that the corporate world expects everyone to become Pied Piper. A quick promotion, some change in the business cards and the expectation that magically everyone around will follow like rats. What gets in the way of leadership is our very definitions and appearances of leaders. When we do think of a leader, we think of a Pied Piper like guy. Unpacking the qualities of the Piper,

- **The mesmerizing musician:** the bright skill sets of a person. He might be great at his job and therefore assumes a leadership role. But the role of a leader is completely different. Every great baker cannot run a successful bakery. Baking a cake requires a single set of skills while running a bakery requires you to lead multiple skills of different people.

- **The charismatic presence:** The Piper had a magical capacity to influence all living beings on Earth. That is the kind of leaders we mistake we need. And we get worried when the company's rats don't jump into the ocean to our tunes. There are two very dangerous situations here:

  - The first one is assuming the Piper will only take away the rats and never our children. This in the business language would translate to a leader who works for his needs much to the disadvantages of all others. This is a toxic leadership situation. Well, Hitler, Napolean and Alexander were able to gather all the followers. But they were all toxic leaders.

  - The second one is thinking the followers should quietly walk behind. This would only create a company full of robots and once they move up the leadership role, they would continue the same tune. In times of uncertainty, this kind of leadership will not help. How many times have you seen people confidently make decisions that have turned out to be disastrous?

- **The bold claim:** The Piper claimed he could eradicate the rats and the king allowed. How many times we have seen a bold vision that turned out to be just a puff of hot air? And, yet, these are the qualities that a leader is touted to have.

The Pied Piper is best left as a fantasy tale, one that kids hear and believe in the magic of the music and the fun but we, as adults, don't try to emulate and manipulate.'

BEING A LEADER IN THE CURRENT TIMES

'What does it then mean to be a leader in the current times—a space in time where the goal is unclear, followers do not want to be led and the top-down leadership is ineffective?'

'The business landscape, as we knew it, has ended and in its place newer fields have entered. For the first time in history, the dynamics of supply and demand have changed. This is not a temporary change; we cannot sit tight and wait it out. The economy will not go back to more demand. We must change the way we do business in this world of permanent excess supply.

'The other paradigm shift comes from the Internet. Information and network on your fingertips. Companies now directly deal with the customers. The Internet has essentially killed stratification in all counts.

'We might be tempted to blame technology for all the changes but it is not just this one factor. The scarcity used to work as a barrier to entry for most companies. Today information, knowledge and, therefore, expertise, labour and raw materials are easily available, and as more people learn, these will become cheaper; thus, the barriers to entry have broken down.

'Business today is at the speed of imitation and if you have the old tactical responses to this by cutting costs, working longer hours, employing cheaper labour, you are only playing up to the law of diminishing returns.

'With such newer shifts, is there a predictable way to succeed in the long term? What does this mean to leadership?

'Arjun, you wanted a leadership masterstroke for the current uncertain times. A masterstroke is something that comes out of the blue and hits a curveball. In leadership, that means the following:

- Do you as a leader have clarity on your field of leadership? What does your field look like? Do you understand the people and their shadows?

- As a leader, do you first practise self-leadership? Are you aware of your shadows and your role in a problem?

- Do you have a clear 360° leadership vision of the future?

- As a leader, can you cultivate a work culture where your team can work towards creating innovative solutions needed to use above the surplus economy?

- As a leader can you look for the source of uncertainty ahead of others, ride that wave and surf the sudden changes?

- Do you own your people by creating a shared vision, building engagement, embracing their diversity to create inclusive systems?

- Do you embrace the chaos and uncertainty around you and adeptly manage the transition to a new path?

- Can you, as a leader, lead in the moment of crisis and use your learnings when it is crucially required of you?'

Arjun listened enraptured by what Ved said. He was sure he would be able to figure out what to do with his issues under Ved's coaching.

'I want to explore how much of leadership I have and what I need to do in future. I have the will to learn and evolve into a better leader and with you here to show the way, it will be a masterstroke.'

Ved then showed him a poster on the wall, a quotation by John Donahoe, 'Leadership is a journey, not a destination. It is a marathon, not a sprint. It is a process, not an outcome.'

Ved then gave a card, plastic one, like the credit cards that read, 'Leadership is a Hero's journey, a path where individuals develop, transform and become leaders.'

On the back of the card was written,

'Your journey awaits....'

ARJUN'S NOTES: MY LEADERSHIP MASTERSTROKE

1. How can I rewrite my leadership narrative?
2. What are the uncertain factors in my industry?
3. How do I find answers to the questions Ved asked?

NOTE AND REFERENCE

1. *Kathāsaritsāgara:* The *Kathāsaritsāgara* or the 'Ocean of the Streams of Stories' is a retelling of Guṇāḍhya's Bṛhatkathā by Somadeva. It is an 11th-century collection of Indian legends, fairy tales and folk tales and includes two major stories' collection among its numerous stories—the *Betaal Pachisi* and the *Panchatantra*. The stories of the *Kathāsaritsāgara* have been the inspiration for the stories of *The Arabian Nights*.

Arjun had questions, some that were clear and that he could articulate in sentences, while others still vague and showed on his face. Last night he had only tossed and turned and slept badly.

Ved had sent him home right after the welcome note. He simply said, 'Your journey begins from tomorrow. Meet me at the cricket stadium by 5 am?'

Arjun knew the stadium. During college, they would work out and play cricket. So here he was, the years have taken the sprint out of him, though he managed a light jog, gasping for breath.

Ved zipped past, his pace a clear indication that he never gave up these runs from college days. After three more laps, Arjun stopped. He had long ago changed the jog to a walk and now dragged himself to the seats.

The sun was yet to rise and the sky had a beautiful pre-dawn glow, the warmth of hope and the expectation of newer possibilities.

Players, runners and kids started pouring in for various workouts. Ved settled next to Arjun, bottles of chilled water in his hand.

Ved waited in silence. He had specifically given the time, both last night and this morning for the doubts, resistance and questions to surface. The human mind is amazing. It constantly strives for something more and remains in this constant state of being a seeker and yet when change is required, the resistance, doubts and negatives worm out like termites.

As expected, Arjun looked up to ask, 'Ved, I have been thinking of the problems I have in my organization, and they stem from different places and different teams, some of which I am not even in direct contact with. How can I solve them all by just changing myself?'

Ved smiled and said, 'I expected you to ask this question Arjun. And that is the reason we are here.'

He turned back to the grounds in front and pointed out, 'Do you remember our games and the inter-college matches?'

Arjun turned towards the grounds. The players had completed their warm-up and had now formed a loose team to play a game. There were around 16–17 boys, not enough for two teams but they managed. It had been the same during their college days too. Arjun had been their opening batsman for two years and team captain for one. He missed those times.

'What does success in the game mean to you?' Ved asked.

Arjun thought for a bit and said, 'Success, of course, means winning a game but when you are playing, winning is only the reflection of your success.

A great team that can play with all kinds of bowlers and batsmen and pitches are important, as you never know whom you will be up against in the next match. So, the first step is the ability of the team. Then the coordination between players, the strategies of the game and even the tactics of field placings are important. When all these things work in order, it is a successful game.'

Ved nodded in agreement. 'I agree with all your points Arjun. Success in a game can be answered in many ways. It is like the story of five blind men hugging an elephant and trying to describe what it is. Whichever part you hold, your definition changes.

'Let us look at it from here, the seats. What do you feel about the game being played?'

'I think the players are still finding their feet and field placements, even the batsman. So many gaps for a boundary but he hasn't figured them out. See that shot? There are so many gaps between gully and cover, but he hit to the fielder positioned near extra cover where the fielder was ready.'

'Arjun, if you were playing there right now, as a batsman and captain what are the things you see?'

Arjun thought for a while. He has been opening batsman and captain and the task was never easy. Finally, he answered. 'It is rather difficult to navigate that time. I am a batsman and a captain. I need to concentrate on my game and also on the game of others. At the time while I am batting, my focus is completely on how to get runs. And yet there is a dichotomy—between the player in me and the captain, between the immediate next run and the longer match, between competition and collaboration in my team and, most importantly, between the strategies and tactics used and the gaps we missed. As a captain, you sometimes are the ball tossed between the ends.'

Ved had this massive smile on his face. 'Exactly my point,' he said. 'You see leadership is best explained in that field. Let me help you.'

He then reached into his bag to get a few sheets of paper. He drew a quick sketch of the ground, marking the pitch, a few players and the boundaries.

'Ok, this is your ground. While you bat, as you say, your focus is on the runs. This can be single or a boundary. This translates to both long-term vision and immediate results.

'The next important place is your team is the people. You cannot succeed without every player being his best. It is also important that they have good dynamics amongst themselves, coordinate their game and complement each other.

And then are the strategies and tactics required for the success of the game itself.

'The pillars of leadership has been explained in numerous theories. The earlier leadership theories like trait, behaviour, transformational, situational and the newer ones of servant, authentic or shared leadership theories has the same common factors, even if their order and interactions vary. The pillars of leadership are:

1. **The goal:** This is the leader's vision of the desired future.

2. **The people:** Team members, their outputs, dynamics, motivation, engagement and growth.

3. The process: All the strategies and tactics used to ensure the people work towards the goal.'

Ved then looked at Arjun, 'Do you want to add anything else?' He asked.

Arjun nodded his head in the negative. 'I guess that just about covers all that we try to do.'

Ved then brought out a neat pair of scissors and started cutting the paper. He cut out the entire area in the centre that was the pitch. Now, he handed over the sketch to Arjun and said, 'This is your game now. What are your strategies to win?'

Arjun looked at the paper and said, 'But you cut out the pitch. How can one play?'

'Let me tell you a story. An often-heard one and therefore I don't know its source; nevertheless, this is my version of the tale.

'A few boys, just short of 14 years, had an exam the next day. They decided to study the night but spent it talking and playing instead. When the first rays of sun hit their windows, they knew it would be impossible to clear the exam.

They decided to prank the school in the hope that exams for the day will be cancelled. They brought in three goats and marked them as 1, 3 and 4. They then left the goats inside the school campus and went back home. A few hours later the watchman came in. He saw one goat near the admin complex. He ran to catch the goat. After some bit of chasing he managed to catch the goat. By then a few other support staff had come in. They saw another goat in the playground. One of them noticed that the goats were numbered.

'So they now had goat 1 and 4. They searched the entire campus and found goat 3 hiding. They called the principal to say that goat 2 was missing. As expected, the school declared a holiday while the staff members searched for goat number 2.

'In that story, there was no goat with the number 2 and yet they searched.

Figure 3.1: *The Donut Leader*

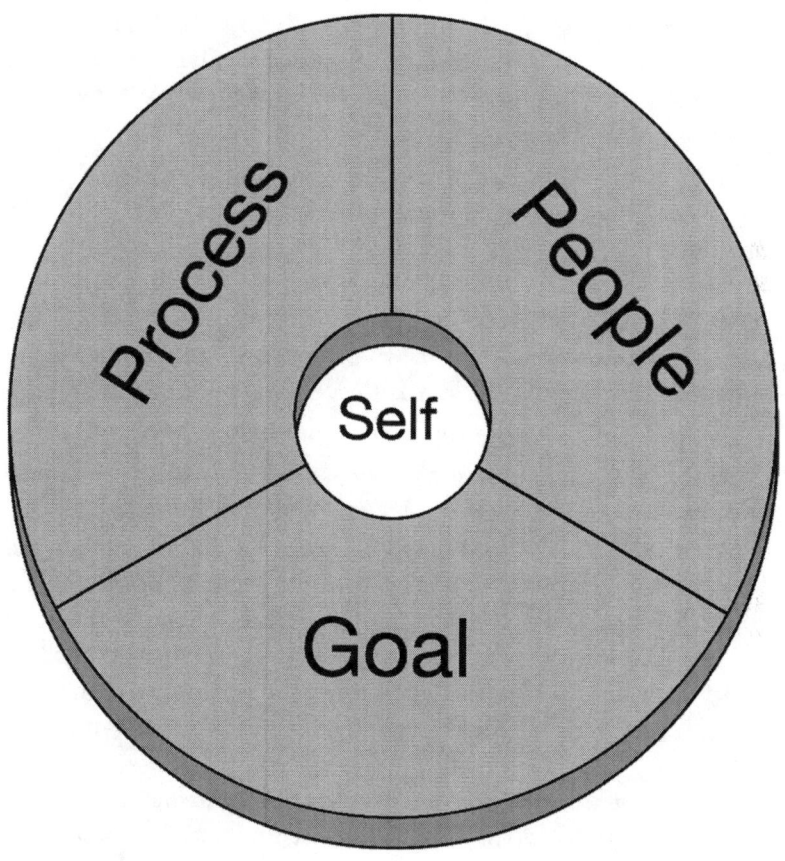

'In leadership, there is a fourth element, which we don't consider. When asked what will be your strategy while playing cricket, you knew there is a dichotomy between the player and the captain. Yet when it comes to the solutions you want the goal, people and process to improve. But there is a huge hole here because you forgot YOU—the player, the leader.'

'Ved quickly pulled out a fresh sheet of paper. His passion for the entire process was so palpable. A few people had stopped to look at us, the heat was rising slowly and the stadium started emptying out. Ved was oblivious to the changes around him. He quickly drew a two-by-two matrix called the field of leadership.

Let us look at the complex picture that forms the field of leadership in current times. There are four basic quadrants in this field—The Goal, The People, The Process and The Self.

'**The first quadrant** is the place where companies operate. Their growth, revenues, profits, the increase to stakeholder value and new products in the marketplace to everything under the world economy comprise the goal.

Currently, this marketplace or business world loves the acronym formulated by the US army—VUCA. The goal quadrant is very dynamic and the unpredictability throws a lot of challenges. This is a tumultuous time for business in general and without a doubt in India. The problems manifest in this quadrant and come to light. We see a breakdown of systems—economic, political or technological; leaders often find themselves ill-equipped to manage change as many times they never move out of this quadrant.

'**The second quadrant** is the process. All strategies and tactics used to achieve the goals of quadrant 1 come here. In these challenging and uncertain times, the right strategies can help create disruption. When the global economy was under the effects of the 2008 financial meltdown, Cadbury India launched Tang, the drink mix and Oreo cookies in India in 2011. Both were successful and Cadbury managed to ride the slowdown. [1]

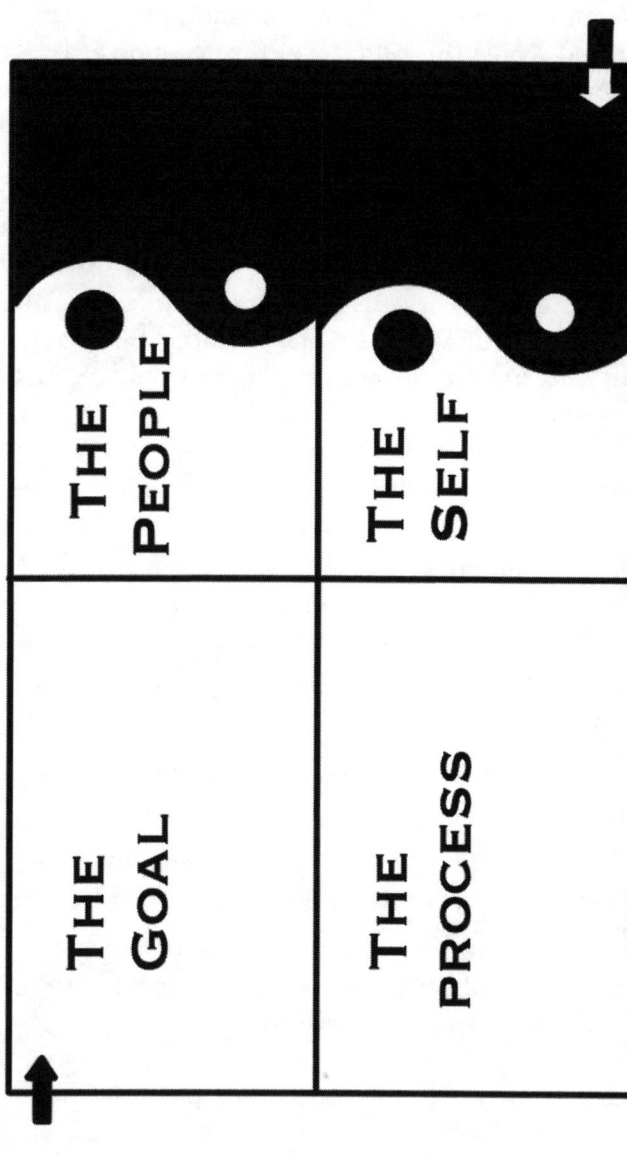

Figure 3.2: *The Field of Leadership*

'Currently, it is the auto industry that is under fire due to rapid changes—the introduction of green electric vehicles and the fluctuating market conditions. Shekar Viswanathan, Vice Chairman and Whole Time Director of Toyota Kirloskar, considers these, and his question is, 'Should auto industry abandon the manufacture of ICE (internal combustion engines) vehicles and focus only on EVs (Electric Vehicles) or should it make both? [2] This is what VUCA means for the automotive industry. Policies, tax rates and customer attitudes favour electric vehicles. This has also made the whole process of decision-making for the auto industry very complex, as customers have turned negative in their approach to ICE vehicles. But the road for EVs is not yet clear. The auto industry is supported by a whole lot of other sectors—the finance, insurance; for EVs there needs to charging stations, skilled labour, after-sales service, etc. Will this function on the best in-demand function that the ICE vehicles currently enjoy?

'The important point to note is that every stakeholder is affected in a VUCA world—only the quantification and timing of the impact is what every stakeholder is grappling with.

'The process involving complex strategies is the leadership need in this quadrant.

'These two quadrants are the more operative side of the business and are addressed with logic, analysis and objectivity.

'The quadrants are divided into strategic, comprising the first two quadrants, and humanistic, comprising the third and fourth quadrant.

'The third and fourth quadrants in comparison are the softer skills, the subjective aspects of leadership.

'**The third quadrant** is the most complex and intangible dimension. This belongs to the people. The entire human element of an organization is here—the way people feel, behave, and work defines the culture.

'In general, people form the culture and culture supports the strategy. But the current complex business world adds global demographic shifts, increasing diversity in thoughts and approaches, migration and virtual teams, changes in life patterns that have shifted motivation concepts and work culture.

'To add to this chaos are the decisions of leaders to offer piecemeal solutions to interconnected problems. Another place leadership fails is mixing objective ways to subjective problems.

'We have heard the popular quote: culture eats strategy for breakfast. Culture supporting strategy is a unidirectional flow between the quadrants. Trying to create a "cultural strategy," that is, bringing in operative tactics to the alive and continuously evolving culture and people - is opening a Pandora box.

'Much like your team's idea to create new increment plans to retain and control performance-based attrition. A problem that exists in quadrant 3 and solutions planned in quadrant 2 will just not cut it.

'Koestenbaum [3] in his book calls them two sides to leadership—objective and subjective. He claims, the two territories have their own languages and logics and that the thinking and the methodology for each are different. 'Outer space requires science; inner space, intuition. The outer world needs measurement; the inner world, poetry.

'**And the last quadrant** is the most neglected and ignored aspect of leadership. Even theories in leadership development cluster around the other three quadrants. "The Self" quadrant is often the neglected Cinderella among the more flamboyant cousins of culture and strategy.

'Paradoxical it may seem, self-leadership precedes strategy and culture. While problems manifest in quadrant 1, the search for their solutions should begin in quadrant 4.

'Self-leadership includes self-awareness, setting goals for self, honouring self, actively rejecting pessimism, and being the change- you want to see in the world. Noda argues [4] in his article

'Leadership Begins with Leading Oneself' that leading oneself is the exact starting point of leadership.' The way you play, the way you lead, the way you deal with others, the way you strategize and the tactics you use are very important. In fact, in leadership, first, lead yourself to lead others. Wholesome leadership means addressing all four areas in the required sequence.

'Or else, you will be a donut leader.'

A DONUT LEADER

'A donut leader is one who does not realize the role he plays both in the problem and in the solution. He takes himself out of the picture by being blind to his role as part of the team, essentially creating a massive hole in the centre of this wholesome field of leadership. By digging a hole due to lack of self-awareness, he becomes a donut leader.

'Surviving in the uncertain world has become the zeitgeist. And yet when the crisis hits the roof, two questions immediately pop out:

1. Who is the boss?

2. Who is to blame?

'For a world that lives in the allure and addiction of selfies, there is very little thought given to the person behind the picture. Being a great leader involves a lot more than becoming an effective manager or a better strategist.

'Fundamentally, leading yourself is the process of personal trans-formation. For a lot of people, the focus is outward, thinking of leadership as being the person in position of authority or the qualities that make a better leader or even the process, other people and strategies.

'Personal transformation is a requirement in leadership and becomes the first step to wholesome leadership in uncertain times. This first step can never be explained better than drawing the analogy to the moment when the great warrior Arjuna in

Mahabharata faced his biggest uncertainty *(dharmasankata)*—to fight his family or put down the arms even before the battle at Kurukshetra began. Such uncertainties are too complex to be solved at quadrants 1 and 2 and require leaders to transcend to a deeper level of awareness in quadrant 4.'

LEADING THE MOST DIFFICULT PERSON—#YOU

'Talleyrand, who was Napoleon's chief diplomat, is known for his crafty, cynical diplomacy. His very famous quote is, "I am more afraid of an army of hundred sheep lead by a lion than an army of hundred lions, led by a sheep."

'Closer home, we have the Ramayana where the mighty king *Ravana* and his entire army is defeated by a simple austere man in exile, Rama, and his army of monkeys. Lord Rama the *Maryada Purushottam* (a man who is supreme in honour) stands for a man who has all 16 prescribed qualities that make for a great human. His story has been an epic in self-discipline and self-management.

'Self-leadership is having the heightened sense of who you are, where you want to be and a clear understanding of your emotions, behaviour, shadows and abilities to get there.'

Arjun had been silent for the entire time. He was beginning to see a larger picture emerge. When he first came to Ved he expected a quick change in strategy and some quick-fix solutions that will fix his immediate gaps. Arjun now understood these quick-fix solutions are the reason new cracks appear in the company's success pipeline. He mused aloud.

'To understand what you are saying, my problems can be in quadrant 1, 2, or 3 but the solutions should always start in quadrant four?

'In short, self-leadership is a path toward more effectively leading others? Like walk your talk and practise what you preach?' Arjun asked.

'Very true', Ved adds. 'Bryant and Kazan [5] define self-Leadership as having a developed sense of who you are, what you can do, and where you are going, coupled with the ability to influence your communication, emotions, and behaviour on the way to getting there. According to Andrew Bryant, self-leadership equates to the leadership competencies of self-observation and self-management but most importantly, self-leadership influences all aspects of your life, your health, your career and your relationships. Self-leaders are self-motivated to take purposeful action and therefore make better leaders, entrepreneurs, and team members.

'Self-leadership involves the integrity of walking your talk, but it is a lot more than speech with integrity—it is the way you see yourself every day, becoming aware of who you are and where you want to be and influencing yourself to get there.'

'So how does one go about grooming self-leaders?' Arjun wanted to know.

Ved looked around him smiling. As expected, a small crowd had formed around listening in rapture to Ved's passionate and deeply insightful speech. At their request, Ved continued, though by now they had moved to the cooler waiting areas in the office block.

LEAD YOURSELF BEFORE YOU LEAD OTHERS

'Let me share an interesting story, this time from Ancient Greek history. This is part of the letters written by Plato. [6]

'In Plato's first trip to Syracuse, he was to help Dionysus I, the Greek tyrant, known for cruelty and rampage strikes, in the art of leading others. Plato could not make him see the ways of leadership and the mission was without much success. Plato was not able to educate him because Dionysus I did not accept Plato's technique of teaching. Dionysus I even threatened to imprison Plato at this stage. Plato returned consequently to Athens and founded *Akademos* in 387 BC, which laid the foundation of the educational system in nowadays world. The main idea of *Akademos* was to educate people to educate themselves.

'The reason why he failed to teach Dionysus and why so many others wanted to learn from him millennia after his death is probably best explained by the Greek lines inscribed above the academy's entrance, a phrase which means "Let none but geometers enter through this door." A leader should thrive to create harmony between his inner and outer respect. He/she should align the realms of respecting oneself with the respect of others and should, therefore, create a balance between those two. Only when the first one is achieved, the latter can follow. "The art of leading others comes through the art of leading oneself."

'Leadership is a Hero's journey, a path where individuals develop, transform and become leaders. Who provided the leadership for successful business people like Bill Gates in founding Microsoft, or to Narayana Murthy to create Infosys? The leadership came from within them.'

'But why is this journey inside oneself so difficult and elusive?' Arjun was thinking about the question when a young woman in the crowd asked Ved.

Ved smiled and answered, 'We all lead ourselves, every day. The point is that you are your own leader, and just like any leader you can be a good one or a bad one. The first maxim on the ancient temple of Apollo by Delphi is *Know Thyself* [7]. The maxim has been talked about by all great philosophers but to answer your particular question, I'll consider lines In Plato's *Philebus* dialogue [8]; Socrates refers back to the same usage of "know thyself" from *Phaedrus* to build an example of the ridiculous for *Protarchus*. Socrates says, as he did in *Phaedrus*, that people make themselves appear ridiculous when they are trying to know obscure things before they know themselves.

'In much the same way, people tend to learn about all things outside than work on themselves on the inside. Leading yourself is not easy. And some of the reasons are:

1. **Blind spots till they blow up:** Individuals are not aware of their measure of themselves and therefore have a lot of blind spots. In his book *Emotional Intelligence*, Daniel Goleman talks of this as the self-awareness.

2. **The long arc of development:** self-leadership is an oath to lifelong development and learning. The path, while most effective, is a long winding narrow lane mostly travelled alone. To the world that requires quick-fix solutions; this long arc does not look like an option worth investing energy in. Also, while the solutions begin with the self, culture and strategy cannot be changed in the short term with the development of self. So self-leadership is the nature's cure, the good health and the prevention mechanism in the life of a company but when the crisis hits, it cannot be used as an antibiotic pill.

3. **Outward measurable indicators:** the outward success indicators that are readily available and immediately for strategy and even team effectiveness are very obscured for self-leadership. What is the measure of a transformed person? That is the satisfaction that only he will have and this means skipping the indicators in Maslow's hierarchy to self-actualization. To a person looking for outward affirmations for his success, the journey into himself does not hold any measurable success indicator. His resistance to delving deeper into himself will be more.

4. **Too harsh on yourself:** A common reason is also we are our worst critics. Being too harsh on oneself and a lack of self-love creates negative energies inside us that hinder the smooth flow of awareness in a neutral setting. Our perceptions will be coloured and the result attacks our self-confidence. Again, the process of self-leadership is hampered beyond this point. Like Agnes Repplier says, "It is not easy to find happiness in ourselves, and it is not possible to find it elsewhere."

'The concept of self-leadership is derived primarily from research and theory and according to Charles Manz [9], who has done extensive research in the field and published numerous books and research papers in the topic, self-leadership is derived from self-regulation theory, social cognitive theory, self-management, intrinsic motivation theory, and positive psychology.'

Arjun, who was deeply pondering on the diagram of the four quadrants suddenly asked. 'Ved, the quadrants 3 and 4 have this yin-and-yang kind of black and white in them. What do they stand for?'

'That my friend is a very deep lesson, better saved for tomorrow evening. Before we leave, I would like to leave you all with a few questions to ponder as you take the inner journey to leadership.

1. What does "leading thyself" mean to you?

2. Why is it important to lead myself?

3. How can I rewrite my leadership narrative?

4. What must you really know to run a successful enterprise?

5. What must you understand to be an effective leader?

6. How will you "grow the business?"

7. How can you improve quality and productivity?'

The crowd slowly moved out, some discussing their views, others in simple friendly chats thanking Ved for his impromptu session.

As they parted, Ved gave Arjun a fresh diagram of the four quadrants. 'Arjun, treat this like a blueprint. You can superimpose the four quadrants to any company and crisis. Before we meet tomorrow, put all your problems into the four quadrants.

Defining the problem clearly solves half the problem.'

REFERENCES

1. Karnik M. Strategies for a VUCA world. Available from: https://www.livemint.com/Specials/bmBOBB3PMTVhz4EQsMZphK/Strategies-for-a-VUCA-world.html

2. Auto industry in the VUCA world. Available from: https://www.et-ilc.com/members-in-media/volatility-uncertainty-complexity-and-ambiguity/

3. Koestenbaum P. *Leadership, the inner side of greatness, a philosophy for leaders*. San Francisco, CA: Jossey-Bass; 2002.

4. Noda T. *Leadership in action: In focus - the leadership journey - leadership begins with leading oneself.* Greensboro, NC: Center for Creative Leadership; 2002.

5. Andrew B, Ana K. *Self-leadership: How to become a more successful, efficient, and effective leader from the inside out.* New York, NY: McGraw-Hill Education; 2012.

6. *Epistles*, a set of 13 letters by Plato is a comprehensive work. The part about Dionysus and Academy is written in the seventh letter.

7. Green MS. *Know thyself—the value and limits of self-knowledge.* London: Routledge; 2017.

8. Wikipedia. Know thyself. Wikiwand. Available from: https://www.wikiwand.com/en/Know_thyself

9. Neck CP, Manz CC, Houghton JD. *Self-leadership: The definitive guide to personal excellence.* Singapore: SAGE Publications; 2019.

4   MIRRORS AND SHADOWS

Arjun spent the rest of the day in office. He locked himself up in his room, cancelled his meetings and sat down to work on the four quadrants that Ved had given him.

Arjun was a meticulous and hard-working person. Give him data and a few measurable indices and he was at his best. Arjun was sure he could crack the code to transform his company by the end of the day.

The next five hours flew by. The passage of time left its mark with empty coffee cups and the papers on the desk. After three sheets of hand drawing, Ved's field of leadership, Arjun got 20 photocopies for the many iterations.

First, he listed problems that were visible. Slowly, the issues that showed in the Goal seemed like problems in the Process and many had their roots in the People. He found new problems as the interconnection between the quadrants emerged. Now with numerous arrows, strikes and connections, the quadrants looked like a spider web. Unfortunately, he felt like a moth caught in the spider web instead of the spider that created it.

And this was the chilling realization he had. It was his company, his dream and therefore his spider web. But the empty quadrant 4 shouted with cymbals and drums that maybe all along he has been a donut leader. The spider webs we weave tangle, leaving each strand interconnected in its chaos.

Arjun, of course, did not become the successful CEO walking on the magic carpet. Experience and failures have left deep battle scars on him and the wounds now speak of the determination and grit and a keen vision.

Arjun simply took out another photocopy and decided to work from the Self-quadrant. He wrote for a while but decided that the points looked like the desired changes he felt he wanted instead of the problems that he should have written. Arjun recalled reading the philosopher Alan Watts quote—'Problems that remain persistently insoluble should always be suspected as questions asked in the wrong way, like the problem of cause and effect.' So he decided to write down the issues as questions instead of sentences.

The very act of converting a full stop into a question mark opened the doors for Arjun. He now worked from the space of wonder instead of the limiting space of judgement.

He pondered over the seven questions that Ved had left the group with and slowly began to rework the quadrants.

He managed to complete the entire four quadrants and, now, could not wait to meet Ved the next evening.

The next evening, the friends met at Ved's corporate Vetaal office. Arjun was anxious to find answers to the questions he had written. He came prepared—he brought his laptop where he had a more complex spider web problem map and spaces for the possible solutions.

Arjun rushed in, 'Ved, thanks for that insight, into the field of leadership. I have covered all the issues. Now let's attack one by one and conquer the field. I am so excited.'

Ved looked at the completed sheet and the questions. He smiled, exhaled deeply and said, 'I'm glad to see you so pumped up Arjun, let's sit down and discuss.'

Over cups of hot filter *kaapi*, Ved asked, 'So how do you feel now?'

'Oh, I feel in control. I converted the issues to questions, saw the possibilities and now if we just nail the answers, we can begin implementation.'

'Where were the problems?' Ved asked

'Let me show you.' Arjun brought out the filled-up sheet again but Ved just waved them off.

'On a broad level Arjun, where were the problems?'

Arjun fired up again, 'Many issues in quadrants 2 and 3. I am seeing a lot of connections between them and can link it to the goal quadrant.'

'And now by working on the answers you can solve them all?'

'Yes,' smiled Arjun.

Ved was silent for a few minutes. Arjun began to feel like he left out something important in his analysis. Ved slowly pointed to a potted plant in his office. 'You see that new leaf? Where did it come from?'

Arjun was disappointed. He was expecting to get to the solutions part already. But now they were going to go through another circle. Yet, Arjun trusted Ved a lot. He answered, 'From those branches.'

'Exactly. You know that leaves sprout from branches and birds hatch from eggs but when we talk about us humans, we use a mightier term—we came into this world. We did not come into this world; we came out of it—people living in this world, our parents created us. In just the same way you did not just discover these issues and they did not come into the quadrant of strategy.

'Your current people and strategy created these problems.'

Arjun was shocked. 'How? I do my best to mitigate all problems. Many new ones still sprout but how did I create them?'

'Let us revisit a *Panchatantra* [1] story that we have heard as kids. Do you know the *Panchatantra* tales are called *Neeti sastras* meaning "the ways of life?"'

This story is about the arrogant tyrannical lion that caused widespread fear among the animals in the jungle. He would kill anyone for pleasure or food and called it his right as the king of the jungle.

To mitigate the problem that clearly existed in the personality of the king lion, the animals out of fear came up with the brilliant idea–a strategy to minimize loss. They would send one animal on their own so that the lion will not harm at random. Problems are always easy to live with as long as they don't surprise us. We can imagine the bourgeois underbelly of politics of who should be the next meal in the jungle.

By eliminating the lion as a problem, they just replaced political power as one. Does this sound like India after Independence?

Moving back to the jungle, this situation moved on until one day it was the turn of the rabbit.

The little rabbit decides to work deeper and actually push the lion to quadrant 1. So he arrives late to kindle the anger in the lion and then spins a story of another lion that delayed his trip. Theories in emotional intelligence would explain the brilliance of the rabbit as it waited for hunger and anger to fuel the irrationality in the lion. The rabbit now leads the lion to the well and informs that the lion challenging them is inside. The story, of course, ends with the arrogant lion meeting his image in the waters and attacking its shadow by jumping into the well to drown.

'While for kids, the moral of the story is about the wit of the rabbit, as leaders, we need to see larger life lessons. There are three important ones:

1. Using control measures to solve problems at strategy levels do not help. They only create newer issues.

2. Like the lion, a refusal to meet our shadows makes us toxic and

3. Attacking our shadows will kill us.

'The lesson here is to become aware of the shadow inside us and accept it to rise above it. That lion is present in all of us. Fear and anger at meeting our shadows cause more problems than solutions.'

Arjun thought about the story. 'Does this mean I have managed to write clearer questions in strategy and goal but my unexplored shadow side makes the self and people quadrant look only at the white side?'

'I am curious to know what is a shadow? How do I find mine and, more importantly, what should I do when I do find mine?'

Ved began, 'In science, anything with substance casts a shadow when it comes under the path of light. In the same way, shadow refers to the part of your unconscious psyche that does not want to come to light.

'As much as we want to deny it, we are imperfect human beings and the more we become aware of our imperfections, we become better humans.

'The shadow or imperfections are referred by us in different ways—the dark twin, disowned self, alter ego, etc. We also use a lot of metaphors to describe these shadow encounters—meeting our demons, waging the inner battle, midlife crisis. Carl Jung [2] first gave the term "shadow" to refer to those parts of our consciousness that have been neglected out of fear, ignorance, shame or a lack of love. So shadow is the person you don't want to be.

'Most people would go to great lengths to protect their self-image from unflattering observations. We cannot eliminate the shadow. Trouble is not the shadow but our refusal to acknowledge it.

'We have read the famous story of Robert Lois Stevenson, The strange case of Dr Jekyll and Mr Hyde [3]. The kind-hearted working scientist Dr Jekyll is transformed into a violent and cruel Mr Hyde.'

RECOGNIZE YOUR SHADOWS

'Shadow by its nature does not come to light. It hides in our behaviour, our conversations, our opinions, even in our humour. Poet and author Robert Bly compares our shadow to an invisible bag that we carry around ourselves all our life, adding to the bag, making it heavier.

'It is important to understand that inside us we possess every trait and its polar opposite. Our growth lies in owning and embracing both the dark and light to make us whole. This means each of us embodies all the traits in the universe. A step further is to understand that you contain everything you see in others. There is nothing we see or perceive that we are not.

'Let us understand this concept a bit. If you are inspired by a passionate speech about helping others, it is a reflection of the compassionate nature inside you. In the same way, if someone's anger disturbs you, you are capable of the same anger.

'We involuntarily transfer our own unconscious behaviour onto others. Carl Jung calls this the "projection".

'We project our perceived shortcomings onto others. We say those things to others that we should be saying to ourselves. And this means when we judge others, we are judging ourselves.

'Let me share a story of a client.'

Ishaan had spent his entire adult life being this happy, empathetic and patient person. He hated his father's angry outbursts in the house during his childhood and had vowed never to be like that.

I asked him to recognise and own the deep resentments and anger inside him so that he could finally let go and embrace a better life. Ishaan was proud of his soft nature and did not recognise his shadows of anger.

A few weeks of the coaching went on when one evening Ishaan calls. He was out partying with his friends when one of his friends hinted that Ishaan gets angry quickly. A surprised Ishaan smilingly asked, 'have you ever seen me lose my temper?'

The friends then said to Ishaan that he doesn't need words when he has this angry stare and that silent brooding and sulking treatment.

Ishaan could now suddenly see the shadows of anger lurking inside him. He only showed it differently.

'In such moments of strong feelings, we shift to denial hardly noticing the murderous fantasy or a suicidal thought or even embarrassing greed.

'As a leader, we need to keep in mind that if you see greatness in your team it is your own greatness you see reflected, if you see problems in your team it is a reflection of your problems. English psychoanalyst Molly Tuby [4] suggests six other ways in which, even unknowingly, we meet the shadow every day:

- In our exaggerated feelings about others ("I just can't believe he would do that!" "I don't know how she could wear that outfit!")

- In negative feedback from others who serve as our mirrors ("This is the third time you arrived late without calling me").

- In those interactions in which we continually have the same troubling effect on several different people ("Sam and I both feel that you have not been straightforward with us").

- In our impulsive and inadvertent acts ("Oops, I didn't mean to say that").

- In situations in which we are humiliated ("I'm so ashamed about how he treats me").'

THE SHADOW SIDE OF LEADERSHIP

'For most people, leadership is a positive concept. It is not until scandals and scams hit the breaking news that the public comes to know the whole picture. The 2009 Satyam scandal or the recent one in the Kingfisher Airlines brings to light part of the leadership equation that thrives on and abuses the positional authority of the leader.

'It is not just when "leaders turn bad" but also when leaders undermine the subtle social and psychological factors that good leadership is meant to address. Toxic leaders are ones who are not doing anything illegal. In fact, in their viewpoint, they are working towards the good of the society, but such leaders are unaware of their toxic and shadow side.

Harvard professor, Barbara Kellerman, identifies seven types of shadows or toxicity in leaders [5]. The entire story of Mahabharata is a study of human shadows. Do you see Karna and Arjuna? Bhima and Duryodhana? Yudhishthira and Bhishma? They depict similar skillsets but different attitudes and shadows towards their skills set. In our life and business, we see many of these shadows. Some prominent ones have been discussed further.

INCOMPETENT

'These leaders don't have the motivation or the ability to sustain effective action.

Figure 4.1: *The Shadow Side of Leadership*

'They may lack either emotional or academic intelligence. Sometimes they cannot function under stress or their communication comes out all wrong.

'The incompetency as a shadow can manifest in building a culture that does not mind incompetence. It also has challenges in the followers—the challenge of lack of obligation and the challenge of new ambitions and change.

'Incompetence as a shadow works on the confidence of the leader, and he covers this up by showing authority or by resisting change.

'So team members are challenged with change, new ideas are not easily received and the hierarchal system is insisted upon.

'The awareness of your leadership shadow can be the first step to great leadership. Instead of losing in your shadow, embrace the shadow, leverage it and allow it to show the way.

'In *The Art of War*, Sun Tzu [6] writes that to know your enemy, you must become your enemy. In the case of shadows, the enemy is inside you and it is important to understand and value this shadow.

'Confidence comes from skill. Knowing you have the ability to get things done. An incompetent shadow makes the leader feel like an imposter plagued with self-doubt.

'Perfectionists, who feel they always lack something; comparers, who keep thinking someone is better, etc—all come under the incompetent shadow.

'What happens when you embrace your shadow?'

Aarav is a fifty-five-year-old general manager who has been in the company for more than two decades. He joined as a chartered accountant and slowly rose to head the finance in the organization. He is not tech-savvy and often finds himself in a bind when new innovation in technology is introduced in his organization. Fortunately, he had worked in a chartered accountants' firm. But the last decade has made almost every part of his work online. Nowadays, the managers keep talking about cloud storage and he has no idea what that means.

He loved his job and was worried if he will be displaced with new talent due to his lack of technological skills. Aarav would not bring in anything tech-related unless and until it was a government or a company mandate into his department.

This behaviour created a lot of tension in his team as they figured they had to do a lot more work due to the lack of technology. Once the CFO got to know of the dissent in the team; he spoke with Aarav and paired him with a soft-spoken intern who would assist and also show him the ropes. Aarav was glad to have the assistant and, now, could leverage his strength and reach out to others for his weakness.

'The shadow of self-doubt can be won.'

RIGID

'A leader can be competent but if he is rigid in his views, unyielding and unable to accept new ideas, it becomes difficult to navigate the VUCA times successfully. The rigidity can arise from fear of change or the illusion of security in existing conditions. This does not mean such managers are not effective. They work from the primacy of control. They are great leaders in areas of clear growth. They bring in operational efficiency, follow rules diligently and are often the torchbearers of discipline and structure.

'The challenges are often seen in the followers of a rigid leader when team members with new ideas and the explorers following a rigid leader find his structure stifling.

'Arguments, disagreements, passive-aggressive behaviour are expected when followers want a change and are not satisfied with the status quo.

'This also makes inclusion as a concept very difficult in the organization culture.

'One of the best ways to ease the shadow of rigidity is to bring in a trusted friend to act as a devil's advocate, a constant trusted source that shows a different age eases rigidity.'

Rajesh is the head of operations in a bank. His responsibilities include ensuring the promises made by the bank's brand and sales managers are fulfilled within the ambit of applicable laws and regulations while keeping the costs optimal. He has to ensure the accounts are opened within time, funds-transfer requests are acted upon almost immediately, and loans are disbursed to right people etc.

Rajesh prides himself in being the first one to come to the office in his department and later keeps a record of when his team walks in. He is very specific in his instructions and expects efficient outputs. He is happy if he is able to deliver his output efficiently, every day. Even small deviances in his schedule upset him. He expects meetings to be scheduled in advance, the agenda clear and the time and talk adhered to during the meeting.

In case of any cost overruns, he does not take it kindly if they were not pre-budgeted. Even minute deviances from the structures and pillars he has created cause arguments and Rajesh aggressively sticks to his views.

This creates tension in the newer crowd that are lobbying to work anytime and preferably from home. It also creates tension with changes by the sales or customer-facing units as they need to cater to the dynamic customer needs and most times these are not under the structure of Rajesh.

Coming to terms with the judgemental and rigid shadow side of him helps Rajesh become more approachable to the need of the changing team.

INTEMPERATE

'When a leader shows a lack of self-control, he becomes intemperate. As a leader, he or she can be effective but unhinged control of habits, preferences or temper can cause huge harm to his goal and his followers. A lack of self-control can be hiding a very dynamic personality. Let us remember that every warrior is also a murderer and every fugitive was once a hero to someone.

'Especially, of importance is such a shadow as we live in the wild social marketplace of numerous networking media.

'This is one shadow that can be best brought to light by understanding the first and second lines of Delphi—"know thyself" and "nothing in excess." A clearer self-awareness helps recognize the shadows lurking and a life lived in moderation helps control the extremes.'

Kunal works as the head of digital channels in a large bank. He is a brooding man who looks like he carries the burden of the entire world on his wobbly shoulders. The team knows he also has an alcohol problem. There are rumours of his failing marriage and speculations on divorce. A lot of the team members in the digital channels had been part of the team only for the last five or six years but Kunal has been with the Bank for the last 20 years.

The CFO of the bank, one of Kunal's old bosses remembers him as a dynamic young person who would work long hours, assist anyone and always had a smile on his face. On coaching Kunal, his issues came to light. In December 2008, Kunal was working in sales. There were some server control issues and since the Christmas and New Year period was lean, the work was prolonged. As the sales were lean, Kunal had quite a lot of free time. His very close friend in digital channels was then working on a complex project. Kunal spent his entire month helping his friend out. In 2009 when the recession hit, the bank decided to shut down its sales operations in the country as they would soon merge with another bank. Kunal's entire team lost their jobs in a day. The worst part was his friend in digital channels also lost his job and that profile came to Kunal. In the weeks that came, Kunal received some very hurtful words from his team and friends. He still remembers their despair and tension to run a family or pay college fees. Slowly Kunal took his troubles to alcohol.

What Kunal felt was guilt. His anger stemmed from his inability to do anything for his team and friends. As a dynamic warrior who could give up his lean time to help out a friend, he could not live with the passive way he had to keep quiet when his friends and team members suffered.

His guilt at his inability to control a situation made him lose control of his life.

MARTYR

'Martyrs are people who play the victim card to the fullest. They always feel they have been used and not been given enough limelight. They use their prejudices to create tension in the team.

'Such leaders are rarely appreciative as their shadow of not being appreciated enough comes in their way.

'Martyrs though are very caring people. They are nurturers. They work well with people and are the best supporters. The issues arise when they feel their supportive roles are not given the importance it deserves.'

Sadhna is an HR manager. She is also a mother of two young kids. Sadhna always has a complaint in her conversation. When Rahul in Sales got an award, she said, 'It just doesn't matter how his ways are, as long as they meet the target, they are awarded'.

Sadhna has a deep shadow of not being appreciated enough. She puts in 12-hour days, most days of the week. Even at home, she has to do the lion's share of the work. Yet she feels her family and her team do not appreciate her. Add to it, HR is a function that cannot show a quarterly rise in numbers and even here she is in a support function. Sadhna was tired of being in the supporting, assisting and background roles. She wanted to do something in the forefront.

Talking to her, it became clear she wanted to try to work in sales or marketing. Her supervisors tried a hybrid role, a job rotation for her and this immediately brought out the change in her. Sadhna brought out the natural nurturer in her to the customers she faced and sales rose up a notch.

UNCARING LEADERS

'Uncaring Leaders are those who do not really care about their people or the structures in the organization. They are probably very good at their work. The genius researchers, the mad scientists and the innovators who are happy in their knowledge and inventions. But when it comes to business, these people have no idea how to be leaders.'

'Their genius is in their ideas, their new products or inventions or processes. They may be responsible for a whole lot of intellectual property but when it comes to running a company, they may not be the best.'

Yeshaswini has a passion for making organic products. She has studied organic product making and comes from a family of *Ayurvedic* doctors.

She started small by making organic soaps and oils. Given that her knowledge of the product was very good, her products became very popular as the changes in skin and hair were remarkable.

She tasted success rapidly and in two years she had a team of hundred people working on her products which also had increased to shampoos and creams. She now had exclusive outlets in her city and sold in retail stores in 20 cities.

Sales, distribution and dealer relations became her prominent work and she missed the thrill of creating new products. The venture that she started with a lot of passion now started feeling like a burden. She would often be lost in her lab and her employees had to fend for themselves during a crisis.

Yeshaswini soon realized that her passion for creating would always stand in the way of company operations. She decided to form a core team to manage and even nominated a CEO to lead the growth and her people. She retained her role of founder and had more time in her lab.'

Arjun was fascinated by the portrayal of the shadow and its manifestations in our life. He remembered what Ved had asked while explaining about the donut leader—'How are you part of the problem?'

Now, Arjun had to think about what his shadows were and how they were affecting his organization.

Ved now asks Arjun to go back to his field of leadership.

'Go back to the notes you wrote and find out what kind of organization are you trying to create? Who are your people and do you know their shadows? What shadows do you carry?'

'Can you point out places where you and your team are the cause of the problems? Are there any collective shadows? A strong culture can create a collective shadow when the entire group behaves in a particular way. How does this affect inclusion in your organization?'

ARJUN'S NOTES: MY LEADERSHIP MASTERSTROKE

SHADOWS WE CARRY

What kind of shadows do I carry?

Looking back I may have been a bit rigid. I am a structure-oriented person and thrive on plans and spread sheets. I have recruited my pillars also based on the same skill. Raj in sales is this dynamic person and that was the reason I got him in when we needed that rapid entry into the market. But maybe the dynamic is his shadow. He loses his temper often when the sales targets are not met. He almost carries out his tasks like a military general.

Then there is Mahesh and Vignesh. I am not sure of their shadows but they are both very competent in their fields. Maybe I need to speak with them to understand their thoughts better.

The worrying points are the youngsters who want to do work in a very light and easy way. Is that my shadow speaking? Should I look into the positives of what my interns and new recruits are asking?

WHAT KIND OF ORGANIZATION AM I CREATING?

I was confident in the kind of organization I wanted to create. The thought of what kind have I created now is disturbing. The obsession and passion with which our small group surged forward in the initial years have now plateaued as we grow. It is time I look at the changes needed to create an organization that is rapidly growing.

The other problem is the constant changing borrower and lender psyche. With rapid market dynamics, I need a team that can look at the future disruptions and be ready today. Maybe those guys, the nuts team were right when they brought in that algorithm to tap data to understand customer mindset.

NOTES AND REFERENCES

1. *Panchatantra* is an ancient Indian collection of interrelated animal fables in Sanskrit verse and prose, arranged within a frame story. The author of the stories is believed to be Vishnu Sharma.

2. Jung CG. Phenomenology of the self. In: Campbell, J, editor. *The portable Jung*. New York, NY: The Viking Press; 1951. p. 147.

3. Stevenson RL. *The strange case of Dr Jekyll and Mr Hyde*. Harlow: Longman; 1886

4. Zweig C, Abrams J. *Meeting the shadow: The hidden power of the dark side of human nature*. Los Angeles, CA: Tarcher; 1991.

5. Kellerman B. *The shadow side of leadership*. Thousand Oaks, CA: SAGE Publications; 2020.

6. Tzu S. *The art of war*. Mumbai: Jaico Publishing House; 2010.

THE LEADER'S JOURNEY—MAPPING YOUR NARRATIVE ARC?

Arjun woke up excited. Much before the crack of dawn, he was up and looked forward to the trip today. The last week had been a reflective exercise in understanding the nuances of wholesome leadership.

Yes, it has felt like the Herculean task of cleaning the Augean stables [1]. Hercules' fifth labour by *Eurystheus* was to clean the stables of King Augean in a single day. An impossible task as the king had the largest herd of cattle in Greece. Hercules broke off walls and dug trenches, thereby rerouting the rivers *Alpheus* and *Peneus* to wash out the filth.

In much the same way Ved had dug deep into Arjun's beliefs, thought patterns and shadows to flush out the toxins.

Arjun was packed, ready and eager to unleash the Hero inside him just as Ved's beast—a shiny black Audi—slid in.

'Wow, man! Awesome beast!' Arjun exclaimed.

'What can I say? Meet my shadow side, called vanity. He often masks himself as necessity, sound decision-making or even being pushed by others', smiled Ved.

The friends began their journey to the nearby city of Pondicherry— A South Indian state that carries the lingering colonial hue of the French. From Arjun's apartment, it was a 3-hour drive.

Arjun was eager to unpack his learning and start the process. The drive was exhilarating with the ocean on one side and the city on the other. The sun still an invisible ball beyond the horizon though the early rays cast magnificent purple streaks that the few fluffs of clouds trap, making it a purple lining instead of silver. Like Seth Godin's cow [2], those purple linings look like opportunities to a hopeful mind. Early morning marathon runners, cyclists and bikers made for great journey fellow travellers as Arjun enjoyed just being in the moment, with the sea breeze on his face and a smile in his heart.

LEADERSHIP IS A JOURNEY

Arjun turned towards Ved and said, 'This is how life should be. A great journey with speed, the wind on your face and a great friend to share it with.'

'Life is a journey Arjun, and leadership—definitely an adventure trip.'

'I agree Ved. I remember the quote of the renowned German poet, Rainer Rilke— "There is only one journey. Going inside yourself."'

'I would not like to think of leadership, especially in today's business landscape in as simple terms as that. Self-leadership is the first step in leadership, not the entire journey. We still have to master and lead the other three quadrants in the field of leadership. Leadership, therefore, also includes our ability to influence and collaborate with others in our team, race towards all the factors that cause the disruption and be on top of that curve and achieve our goals.

'Leadership is a multilevel, multidimensional transformational journey from the current state to a desired and better future.

'Let me explain. Let's take the journey we are in right now. We are in a six-lane highway. We have five concurrent dimensions to every leadership journey.

'The first dimension of the journey, of course, is "our destination." This journey is towards a greater experience and focused learning and our destination is my beach house in Pondicherry. The proverb of all roads lead to Rome is great only as long as we want to go to Rome. In leadership, this step is the vision. A clear articulation of a leader's vision is the first dimension in the journey.

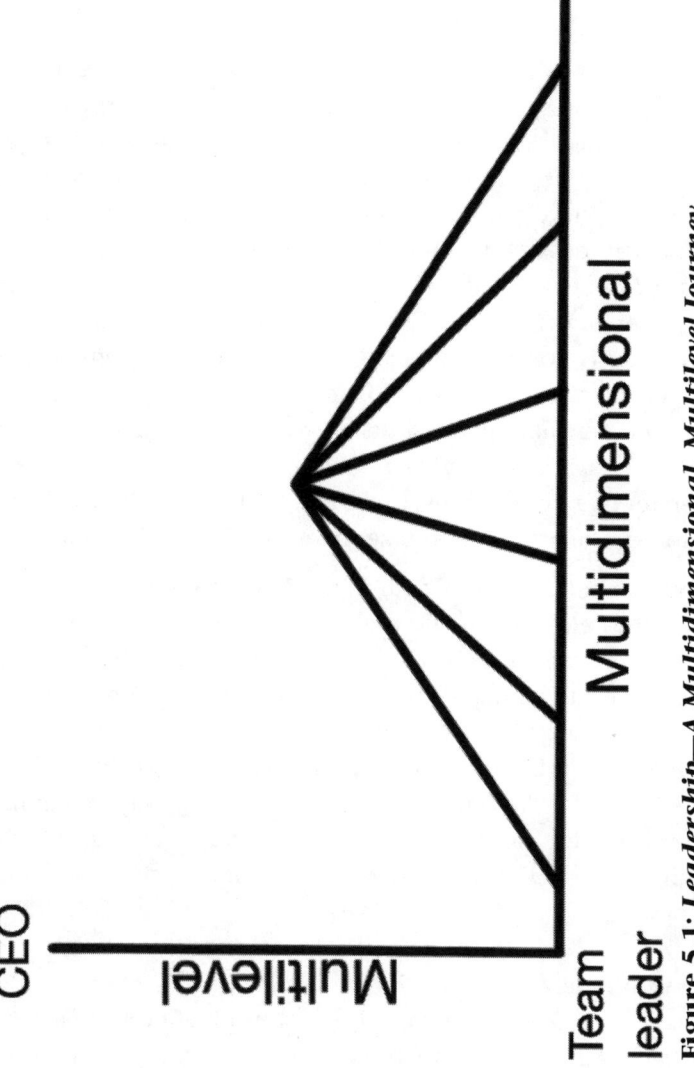

CEO

Multilevel

Multidimensional

Team
leader

Figure 5.1: *Leadership—A Multidimensional, Multilevel Journey*

'The second dimension is "You, the individual." You are travelling, maybe driving. This car, however great its advertisement may make you believe, cannot drive itself. Therefore, you are a very important dimension. The skills of the driver, his emotional balance, his control and joy in the process make the journey what it is.

'The third dimension is all **the other vehicles on the road**. Leadership, in essence, is about navigating this journey with fellow team members, all other stakeholders and the society at large. It is completely possible that our fellow travellers may have different speed levels, different perceptions of risk and completely different attitudes to following road rules. But to ensure the safety of us and others around us, we navigate the journey with eyes open, preferably mouth closed and focused on the road. In the same way, it is completely possible that your team, employees and other stakeholders may not be on the same page as you and maybe their destinations are different too. It is our duty as leaders to find those spaces to navigate, use our skills to either motivate (accelerate) or give space (hit those breaks) manage the conflicts, show the grander vision and take them along the ride.

'The fourth dimension is, of course, **the larger world itself**, the entire ecosystem—the road, the climate, the stops, obstacles, speed breakers and the beautiful sights. These are the external advantages, disadvantages as well as tools and strategies in leadership. In the current VUCA world, it is this dimension that keeps changing. Remember the changing staircases in Hogwarts? (*Harry Potter* series [3]). The current ecosystem is this way dynamic, uncertain and unclear. This dimension currently looks like a drive through the fog-filled uneven terrain without clear roads and markings.

'Leadership is not just multidimensional, but it is multilevel as well. Ram Charan calls this the leadership pipeline [4]. Driving in a narrow lane is different from a drive on a highway or an offroad adventure into the wilderness It requires different skills and tyres for an offload adventure into the wilderness or a sand dune compared to the everyday drive in chock a block city traffic requires us to shed our rush in adrenalin, our pride in the acceleration speed of our beast and tests our patience to drive at a snail's pace, it is the same for leadership. Leadership is a multidimensional journey as a team leader but completely different from the multidimensional journey of a CEO. They are also different for a start-up, a mid-sized company and a large corporation.

'Leadership my friend is one dynamic adventure ride.'

Arjun was awed. 'That is a massively comprehensive and complete outlook on leadership. Most of the time we only look at a part of this perspective and define it based on our limited vision. Truly it is time we change this leadership definition. A better definition for the current uncertain times is—"Leadership is a multilevel, multidimensional transformational journey from the current state to a desired and better future."

'As we drive, what do you think makes this journey great?'

Arjun closed his eyes, a smile playing on the corners of his lips.

'I love the entire picture. The salty breeze that hits my face, the sun rising from the shimmering depths of the ocean, the cool long stretch of the beach to one side and the mundane shops, houses and life on the other side of the road. Oh, I love to watch the runners pound the road, their sweat and determination eating up the miles and yes as Robert Frost says, "I have many more miles of this journey before I sleep."'

'The beauty of the journey lies in the complete picture. Look at the larger leadership journey as a tapestry woven with fine threads to create something rich with meaning and hope. When looked in isolation, the threads may just be an overlapped confusing mess, but as a whole, the tapestry brings in the myriad of colours and the overlapping threads start to make sense.

'If we looked at the entire experience of leadership from a linear unidimensional lens to say the number of miles covered and the milestones passed,'

'Specifically, in this age of innovation where the business landscape is defined by its unstable and ambiguous nature with increasing variety, disruptions and digitization, we need to remember the wise caterpillar in Carroll's *Alice in Wonderland* [5].

'Who are YOU?' said the Caterpillar.

This was not an encouraging opening for a conversation. Alice replied, rather shyly, 'I—I hardly know, sir, just at present—at least I know who I WAS when I got up this morning, but I think I must have been changed several times since then.'

'What do you mean by that?' said the Caterpillar sternly. 'Explain yourself!'

'I can't explain MYSELF, I'm afraid, sir' said Alice, "because I'm not myself, you see.'

'I don't see,' said the Caterpillar.

'I'm afraid I can't put it more clearly," Alice replied very politely, "for I can't understand it myself, to begin with; and being so many different sizes in a day is very confusing.'

'It isn't,' said the Caterpillar.

'Well, perhaps you haven't found it so yet,' said Alice; 'but when you have to turn into a chrysalis—you will someday, you know—and then after that into a butterfly, I should think you'll feel it a little queer, won't you?'

'Not a bit,' said the Caterpillar.

'As Alice says, it is rather difficult to go through so many changes and still remain in control and that is what happens if we look at leadership as milestones in the journey.

'However, look at the entire change, awareness, growth, mistakes, people and ecosystem as a multi-layered tapestry and move milestones to Masterstrokes—A journey to reinvent leadership for the current times.

'We have established that leadership is a journey. The question is how to travel safely to the desired outcome? Who is the hero in this quest? What does success in the quest mean?

'Masterstrokes is essentially mastering the seven-step model to rewrite your leadership story—STROKES. Taking the lessons from Jungian principles and archetypes, the rich lessons in ancient Indian texts and research in the current business landscape, this is a possible wholesome outlook to leadership today.'

They had come into Pondicherry. The lanes grew smaller and traffic heavier.

Ved reached to the back seat to get a square envelope in royal purple. It had the name Arjun written in bold strokes.

'Go on open it,' said Ved.

Inside was a small square mounted canvas of about 3×3 inches. Like a diamond, the canvas had an amazing painting of a bow and arrow. It was intricate in details using the mandala style and yet the whole art itself looked a bit abstract.

Arjun was intrigued. He turned towards Ved to ask him what the painting and the symbols meant, 'Your destination is on your left', and the woman on his GPS announced just as Ved turned left into a French-style beach house. 'Destination arrived'.

For the moment Arjun forgot about his bow and arrow and looked at the beach house in front of him. French designs meshed with antique Indian carvings. A riot of flowers greeted them at the driveway. The lopsided Vetaal with his warning hung outside the ornate doors.

'You have a beautiful place here Ved', Arjun remarked as he got out of the car and walked in soaking the sweet-scented air that held the fragrance of the garden and the bite of sea salt.

'This beach house was built by my grandfather. My dad has some of the best memories of a great childhood in this place. Work and life took him to various cities and countries and now he prefers to retire in colder climates.'

'I have always loved this house and a few years back converted this place into a boot camp retreat for leaders like you. Come on in. Meet Murugan. He and his wife Sarada manage the house.' Murugan was a middle-aged guy with a pleasant smile.'

'You must be tired and we did not stop for breakfast. Let's meet for Sarada's mouth-watering brunch in an hour?' Ved asked.

Arjun was thrilled. 'Can't wait to start this journey deep into myself Ved,' he said holding on to the bow and arrow canvas tightly.

The house was built on two floors. The upper floor looked recently renovated and carried a newer look while the ground floor retained the cosy feel of a place well lived with happy memories.

Murugan had set the table on the terrace that had the gallery view of the vast ocean in front. While Arjun was getting restless to continue the conversation, Ved simply enjoyed the food and the experience. The brunch was cooked to perfection. Arjun had never eaten such tasty quiche with mushrooms and cheese exploding in his mouth with every forkful of the dish.

After that leisurely brunch, they moved to what Ved calls his haunt. A large room right out of the pages of some very creative magazine stood in front of them.

Arjun entered the room stepping on a mat that declared—'All are mad here', with the Alice in Wonderland cat in neon pink.

Abstract art hung on the walls, in vibrant colours and emotions. Clearly, Ved expressed through his brush. One entire wall was filled from floor to ceiling with books. Long French windows led them to the terrace they had come from. The room itself was furnished with rugs, carpets and floor cushions so soft that you just sink into it.

Ved settled on some cushions while Arjun looked at the paintings. He found the bow and arrow among others and it brought him back to his journey.

'I love this place' declared Arjun as he sat down on a few cushions. 'Do you think you missed your calling as a painter?'

'Thanks', laughed Ved. 'So let's get back to that painting, the one in your hand.'

Ved sat up straighter. Gone was the light-hearted smile. Instead was the corporate Vetaal with deep gaze and he asked, 'Look into that painting carefully and describe what you see?'

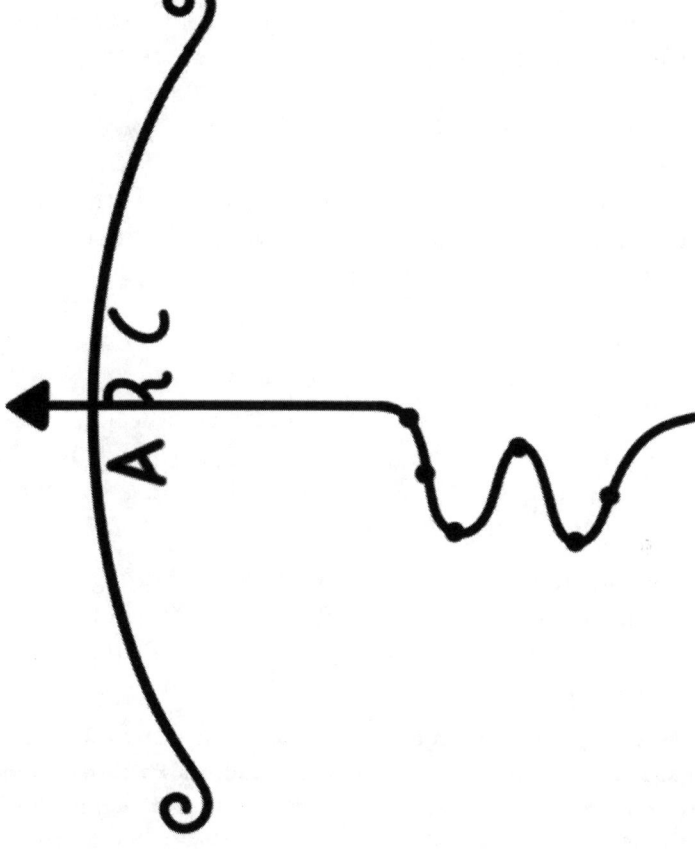

Figure 5.2: The ARC of Leadership

Arjun immediately replied, 'A bow and an arrow. The bow is a broad stroke of paint like a rainbow and has the words ARC written on it. The arrow looks like a meandering river with only the tip straight and pointed. There are seven points on the arrow.'

'Very well explained Arjun. This painting represents the ARC of leadership. The four quadrants define our issues and now if we place this on the field of leadership we get a route map to the journey and the ways to get there.'

THE ARC OF LEADERSHIP

'The ARC on the bow is the broad mindset required and the seven steps in the arrow can be considered as the stops in the journey towards a destination of the desired future.'

THE A IS FOR AWARENESS

'To be aware is to be conscious of the fundamental realities that affect and influence our lives and also people around us. For leaders, it is a quality they need to consciously cultivate as they journey through their life and career.

'Awareness for a leader is an ever-growing and expanding experience. The first roar of awareness can be an 'aha' moment to many like the young tiger cub. There are many versions of this story and this version is mine.

Once a very pregnant tiger is on a hunt. She comes across a herd of sheep on the edge of the forest. She races towards the herd but misses the low iron fence. As she trips, she dies giving birth to a cub. The sheep take the cub with them and slowly the tiger cub is raised eating grass, hiding among the bushes and staying close to the herd.

'It can be the hand of fate or the call of adventure but one day the cub decides to cross the dreaded fence and enter the dangerous jungle. Nibbling on grass, he comes face to face with a ferocious tiger.

'The cub is frightened but the tiger is shocked. "What are you doing?" Roared the tiger.

"I am sorry, I was just nibbling on my lunch" replied a scared cub.

"Why are you eating grass?"

"Coz I'm a sheep and we eat grass."

'The surprised tiger then takes the cub to his cave and gave him some meat. You are a tiger. Like me. Now eat.

'The cub eats meat for the first time and feels that zing on his palate. His claws stretch and he widens his mouth and lets out a roar. Not a big one, but this little roar is the cub's first roar of awareness of who he is.

'The Leadership journey is a journey that begins with the expanding awareness as leaders experience and deepen their understanding of self and also their influence over others. This is critically important to major issues that may either be lost in the noise or buried in the shadow. I am of the view that when leaders fail to become aware, or their awareness is inadequate, they fail to lead effectively.

'Daniel Goleman refers to a "triad of awareness" [6] where he brings attention to "focusing on yourself, focusing on others and focusing on the wider world."

'The triad complements our field of leadership and like Goleman says, "every leader needs to cultivate this triad of awareness, in abundance and in the proper balance, because a failure to focus inward leaves you rudderless, a failure to focus on others renders you clueless, and a failure to focus outward may leave you blindsided."

'In the world characterized by increasing volatility and complexity, leaders need to keep pace with change. Awareness broadens our gaze and widens the playing field. Keeping in line with the multi-dimensions of leadership is an awareness of the increasing interdependence among people, process, goal and the world at large, and the complexity in leadership journey becomes a survival skill.

'Gian Carlo Menotti, [7] the Italian American composer, summed this dilemma aptly when he said; "A man only becomes wise when he begins to calculate the approximate depth of his ignorance."'

THE R STANDS FOR RESILIENCE: ADAPTIVE RESILIENCE

'A significant distinction in any organization reaching peak levels of performance is that they have resilience. More specifically, adaptive resilience. Adaptive resilience is when an individual, team and organization retains the capacity to be productive, resourceful, creative and true to their core purpose while dealing with disruptive forces and adapting with integrity in response to changing circumstances. Walker and Salt define resilience as, "The capacity of a system to absorb disturbance and re-organize while undergoing change so as to still retain essentially the same function, structure, identity and "feedback" [8].

'Like Robert Jorden says in *The Fires of Heaven*—"The oak fought the wind and was broken, the willow bent when it must and survived" [9].

'A cornerstone in your journey as a leader in disruptive times is your ability to harness and build on your adaptive resilience. There are a lot of disruptive forces at play in your industry today—the profile of borrowers, the need for deeper pockets in your lenders, the bullish attitude of the market to the growing sector, government rules, etc. And yet, you are also considered a disruption to the traditional banking sector.'

Arjun had a moment of pride looking back at the journey he had taken to start on his dream, growing steadily every year.

'When the storm of disruption hits, it may sound prudent to resist and hold your ground or even hide behind a boulder. You may emerge on the other side alive but you have not allowed the experience to help you grow or develop. Therefore, resistance to the old is at best a quick fix solution. Instead, think how it might be if you allowed yourself to be engulfed by the storm like Dorothy in the *Wizard of Oz* [10], you may be in for a magical ride to growth and leadership.

'Plato's *Allegory of the Cave* is an apt description of the resistance inside us to adaptive resilience. You can see it all around you; the papers carry massive news of efforts to resist change and disruption regularly.

'The UN videos of disaster-resilient societies exemplify this focus "Jakarta, Indonesia: A City in Jeopardy" [11] depicts a Jakarta neighbourhood facing recurrent killer floods—resulting in, we are told, development issues such as waste-management problems, overpopulation, and unplanned construction, exacerbated by climate change. Speaking through a translator, one man describes the increasing frequency of floods (up to twice weekly), and a woman describes the death of her son by drowning. The video features clips of flooded neighbourhoods, with people wading up to their armpits and even attempting to ride bikes through streets submerged in murky brown water. All appear to be doing what they can to go about their daily lives despite the flooding. This response, we are told by the invisible authoritative voice, is something that the UN and other agencies are working to change. A Red Cross worker explains that they are "teaching [people] that this is not an ordinary situation that they have to accept.... One problem faced by the authorities here is that many people are often willing to accept even extreme risk rather than being relocated to safer grounds." So building a resilient society, in this instance, involves not just changes to building construction or drainage systems but also shifting a culture of fatalism to one of energetic adaptability.

'Adaptation is a cycle nested in a hierarchy across time and space. Sometimes it's fast, sometimes agonizingly slow, can be for just a company or industry or the entire humanity. Adaptive resilience is not a step-wise process but, like awareness, it is a mindset to imbibe.'

THE C IS FOR CURIOSITY

'While the mindsets of awareness and resilience help you wade the storm, it is in the mindset of curiosity that new boats will be built and set to sail on unchartered territories. That impulse to seek new knowledge, the wonder in exploring new possibilities— that is curiosity. Curiosity is the most important mindset that a leader can develop today. When one's curiosity is triggered, we look at possibilities, solutions, and embrace the whole situation problems and all.

'Besides, we live in this age of innovation and curiosity generates those ideas that are the success requirements today.

'To add to it, a curious leader would model inquisitiveness and create a culture based on curiosity and innovation. This builds a sense of freedom among the emerging generation and, in turn, increases their trust and loyalty levels.

'In 2000, when Greg Dyke had been named director-general of the BBC but hadn't yet assumed the position, he spent five months visiting the BBC's major locations, assembling the staff at each stop. Employees expected a long presentation but instead got a simple question: "What is the one thing I should do to make things better for you?" Dyke would listen carefully and then ask, "What is the one thing I should do to make things better for our viewers and listeners?"

'By asking questions and genuinely listening to the responses, Dyke modelled the importance of those behaviours [12].

'But while many want to be curious, not many are. Exploration involves questioning the as is and many actually find that threatening. Efficiency is another detriment of curiosity. The very premise of experimentation is a chance at failure. This translates to the cost of resources and the doorkeepers of efficiency would object to such a waste.'

THE MINDSET CHECK

'You now have the license to use and lead in the ARC mindset,' declared Ved.

Arjun was overjoyed. A ceremonial applause ended with Ved saying, 'Now let us do a quick check on where we are. Let us now unpack those questions you have come up with and analyse them'.

'A rudimentary and preliminary way to check our mindsets is the kind of questions we ask. Look at the questions you have asked in the field of leadership and categorize them as questions starting with why, what about, how and what if.'

Arjun quickly scanned his questions and tallied the scores. There were a lot of questions in 'what' followed by 'how' and 'why' and just one question in 'what if'.

Ved looked at the tallied scores.

He started with the questions. 'The way a question is asked not only changes the answers we get but also tells us where our focus is. So questions that start with "why" are the feeblest. They concentrate on the problems and the details of the problem. Such questions will make the answers orbit around the present reality and never shoot out to the realm of the solution.

'The next set of questions are the "what about" questions; they create awareness in the situation. These questions enable us to explore deeper into the situation.

'The "how"' is a question of possibility. It is a future-looking question and when asked correctly taps into the adaptive mindset of the leader.

'The best questions are of course the ones asked in curiosity— the "what ifs" are the ticket to the Shakespearean unpathed waters, undreamed shores.

If you have a concentration of questions on particular quadrants, you know your mindset in that dimension.'

ARJUN'S DIARY: MY LEADERSHIP MASTERSTROKE

1. What is the traffic in my lane of leadership?
2. What are the 'leader–follower' dynamics of the different dimensions in my leadership?
3. How much of my companies' problems are because my leaders are not leading to their level correctly? How can I implement multilevel leadership smoothly?
4. In all my behaviour, decisions and activities, am I following the ARC of leadership?

REFERENCES

1. To clean the stables of King Augean is the fifth task of twelve labours of Hercules. Available from: https://en.wikipedia.org/wiki/Labours_of_Hercules
2. Godin S. *Purple cow: Transform your business by being remarkable.* London: Penguin; 2005.
3. Hogwarts is the school of witchcraft and wizardry in the *Harry Potter* Series by J. K. Rowling. The schools' staircases keep moving.
4. Charan R, Drotter S, James N. *The leadership pipeline: How to build the leadership powered company.* Hoboken, NJ: John Wiley & Sons; 2011.
5. Caroll L. *Alice's adventures in wonderland.* London: Macmillan; 1865.
6. Goldman D. The focused leader. Harv Bus Rev. 2013 Dec.
7. Menotti GC. BrainyQuote. https://www.brainyquote.com/quotes/gian_carlo_menotti_115993
8. Walker BH, Abel N, Anderies JM, Ryan P. Resilience, adaptability, and transformability in the Goulburn-Broken Catchment, Australia. Ecol Soc. 2009;14(1):12. Available from: http://www.ecologyandsociety.org/vol14/iss1/ art12/

9. Jorden R. *The fires of heaven (The Wheel of Time, Book 5)*. New York, NY: Tor Fantasy; 1994.

10. Dorothy is the main character in the fantasy book from L. Frank Baum's 1900 children's fantasy novel, *The Wizard of Oz*.

11. Obrien S. Resilience stories: Narratives of adaptation, refusal, and compromise. Resil J Environ Humanit. 2017; 4(2–3):43–65.

12. Gino F. Why curiosity matters. Harv Bus Rev. 2018 Oct.

PART 2

The Journey

⌐6⌐   SCRIPT YOUR LEADERSHIP NARRATIVE

The beach looked golden. There is something magical in watching the sun rise from the depths of the sea. The elements that in nature work against each other, the water that extinguishes the fire, work in synergy at sunrise as the ocean from its deepest depths sets free a mesmerizing ball of fire. Every Sunrise is a miracle and a hope; it is such magnificence that triggers deep and powerful verses in poets and philosophers. Arjun, on the other hand, wondered why he never thought of the sunrise in such profound ways earlier, but right now the beach and the morning feels magical.

'Thinking deep?' Ved asked, breaking his run to walk alongside Arjun.

'Ved, right now I feel like those runners way back in 1954 after Roger Bannister [1] busted through the four-minute barrier, ran his mile in three minutes fifty-nine and three-fourths second. British journalist and runner, John Bryant records that prior to Bannister, runners had been chasing the goal since 1886. Coaches and experts believed they had calculated the precise conditions, the kind of track and even the fitness specifications of runners who could achieve this feat. Bannister broke all their myths.

'And then, just a year later, three more runners have conquered the barrier and in the last 50 years over a thousand runners have crossed the elusive four-minute mark. How could so many runners conquer the four-minute mile after Bannister did it when they could not accomplish it before? What makes Roger Bannister the new normal?

'It is the same place I feel I am in right now. I see leadership and all its complexities and there is a sense of calm in me. Your concepts of field and map of leadership had the Bannister effect in me. Now I wonder what is my four-minute mile?

'More importantly I wonder why like all those runners before Bannister, I never saw the possibilities before? '

'I am reminded of M. Ferguson's quote,' Ved said, 'It is not that we are so fearful of the change, or are so endeared with the current. It is the place in between that we fear most: there is nothing to hold onto.

'It is this mental mode that overlooks possibilities and growth. Let me share a story':

As the tale goes, many years ago in the far-off city by the desert a traveller walks in. The city greets him with a gloom so thick that the dusty desert air feels crisp. As he moves inside the city and mingles with the people, he only sees lost hope. People here go about their daily life but life itself was lacking. The soul of the city was lost and the traveller wanted to know why. In a hut at the edge of the city lived an old man whose were the only eyes that sparked, dying embers maybe but it still held the only fire in the city. The traveller asks about the people and the old man says, 'They failed to get to the tree of dreams. If someone succeeds then the people will be better again.'

The traveller decides to go to this tree of dreams and sets off on his journey across the desert with the warning of the old man, 'beware of the shiny casino'.

As the hours go by, the traveller sees a beautiful building in the middle of the desert. He drags his tired self over to the building only to realize it is the casino that the old man spoke of.

He was too tired and the place was too welcoming to not enter. Soon the traveller is sucked into the casino and he forgets why he came there.

You see the casino has four doorkeepers. They are very powerful but deceptive in their appearance. The four doorkeepers are:

1. The allure of comfort

2. The paralysis of fear

3. The addiction to distraction and

4. The power of victimhood

The four doorkeepers work in perfect synergy at the casino. The minute a traveller enters the doors, allure of comfort caters to him. She is soft, polite and makes the guest feel completely at home. She gives the feelings of safety and comfort and slowly travellers forget their call to adventure. The addiction to distraction is her biggest support. Along with secure feeling, distraction now tries to keep guests engaged in the never-ending options of games, lights and glitter. Travellers are hypnotised by the sense of fun, their senses over-whelmed with the options. The minute any traveller remembers of a world outside, the paralysis of fear holds him in. They feel this absolute terror to return to the harsh desert when comfort is easily available here. To ensure the travellers do not feel guilty in their comfortable existence, victimhood gives them the illusionary power to blame any-thing other than themselves.

In this way the travellers stay in the casino for a very long time.

In fact the casino exists for a reason. The place belongs to the tree, the one that the travellers seek. Only unlike the legend, the tree does not hand out dreams; it collects the dreams of all lost travellers. She is the tree of lost dreams. Once a traveller loses his dream, the casino simply throw them out and the traveller goes back to the city, an empty shell.

'What will make you as a traveller to beat the four doorkeepers to the casino called inertia?'

Arjun smiles. 'Wow that was such a powerful story. I could almost feel the tree reach out her long branches to tear away my dreams as I watch helplessly. I think the first step would be to understand the four doorkeepers better'

'In 1971, two brothers opened a bookstore in Ann Arbor, Michigan. In the next two decades their bookstore, the Borders, grew up to become a chain of 650 stores. In 1995, they put out their IPO and growth continued. But in 16 years' time, they filed for bankruptcy [2].

'Just a few years short of the time, Borders announced their IPO, in 1992 in India the Crossword bookstore opened. The bookstore

Figure 6.1: *The Doorkeepers of Inertia*

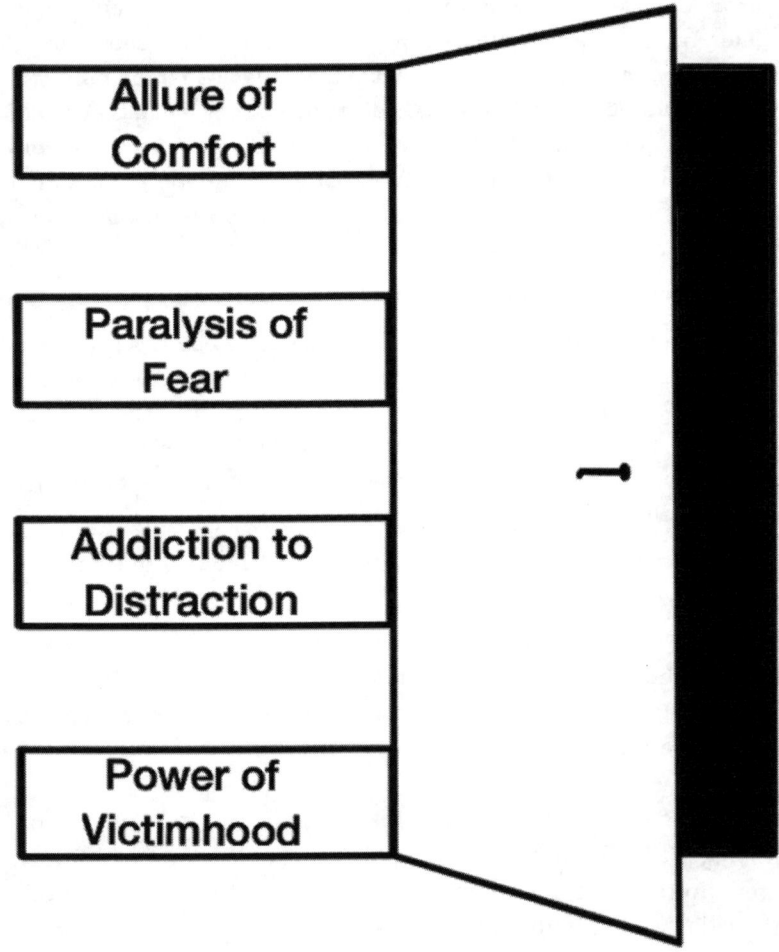

last year celebrated their 27 years in business and continues to grow [3]. Yes, Amazon and the Internet in general has been a disruptor in this industry. The reading habit is also waning but Crossword continues to grow. They have moved from being just a neighbourhood bookstore to sponsoring the Crossword Awards. In short they did not rest in the comfort of their growth.

'This comfort is everywhere around you.

'It's in that warm bed that you don't want to get out of early morning to run.

'It's the Candy Crush you keep swiping at to avoid something more important.

'It's in the job that is safe and stops you from taking the plunge into the deep waters of entrepreneurship.

'It's staying home, doing what you know, and being in the cotton wool wrapped security of the known instead of doing something new and unknown

'Like Robin Sharma says, "The seduction of safety is 100 times more dangerous to the greatness within you than the illusion of uncertainty. Run to your fears. Go to your edges. Hug your monsters" [4].

'The safe zone feels nice but in the long run (or in the short run as the world is changing faster nowadays), it is more dangerous. Our brains are designed to help us stay safe, by predicting or identifying threats. So, the better you identify the threats or risks, the better you can manage them, leading to better safety.

'Seduction means letting go of control of oneself, and that is an illogical thing to do according to the brain (because peace comes from being in control of ourselves and our environment). So, "seduction of safety" would mean giving up safety.

'Also in our minds, we are always asking questions to ourselves only to try and find their answers later and in the process understand our reality better, that is, better perceive the relevant risks and rewards involved in our activities. So, understanding of the risks shapes our perception.

'How do we move out of the safe zone? How do we fight those four doorkeepers?

'The illusion in leadership is that understanding its constituents automatically will make you a better leader. That is like saying reading a "how to manual" on driving or swimming will make us racers and swimming champions. To become the leader you are meant to be, you need to understand that the field of leadership is not the journey. Leadership is largely bound to the theories of personalities, traits, behaviours and the actions that leaders take. and this distillation in theories somewhere makes it inadequate for us to see leadership as a whole.'

THE FIELD IS NOT THE JOURNEY

'The field of leadership might show all the points required for us to travel like a "what's interesting in this place" on a map. Like a typical map that shows us places of interest, petrol pumps and hospitals, a field of leadership shows us the important factors such as the four quadrants, the shadows in people, and the inertia casino.

'A map cannot automatically become the territory. A map of a treasure hunt is exciting, but the journey itself can be arduous and requires a lot more out of us than merely reading the map. This distinction was first represented by Korzybski, representing his view that a simplification or an abstraction derived from something is not the thing itself. "A map is not the territory it represents, but, if correct, it has a similar structure to the territory, which accounts for its usefulness." This concept means that when we view a representation, it is far too easy to confuse the model of reality (the map) with the reality itself (the territory).

'Consider the next steps in leadership in the same way.

'An understanding of the field of leadership is an understanding of the manual and now we need to move towards the actual journey.

'Remember your question when we were discussing the donut leader? Now is the time to answer that.'

Arjun asked, 'You mean while explaining self-leadership I asked how can we action the leading ourselves concept?'

'That is what you have asked now isn't it? How could Bannister do it? What can you do to get out of the casino of inertia? Well now we know. Scripting your leadership narrative is the only way out of the casino.'

WHY AND WHAT IS A LEADERSHIP NARRATIVE?

'Your leadership narrative is your representation of what leadership means to you and what kind of leader you are.

'Imagine recruiting someone for a job. What process is involved? Candidates submit their resumes, go through a few rounds of selection process and are selected. What is your application process as a leader?

'Can you also write a resume? Of course, every leader can but will the resume actually showcase the leader you are? Leadership calls for a different approach.

'Time and time again most leaders have said that they found their leadership by mining their life stories. We are a patchwork of our experiences and actions. Therefore, leadership can be found only by unpacking our fundamentals.

'As a leader though, we are not just a set of traits, awards, skills and jobs on a resume. And that is why the leadership narrative is important.

'It is an invitation for every leader to view their leadership as a narrative journey and script their leadership narrative. The stories we tell ourselves help us make meaning out of our actions and life.

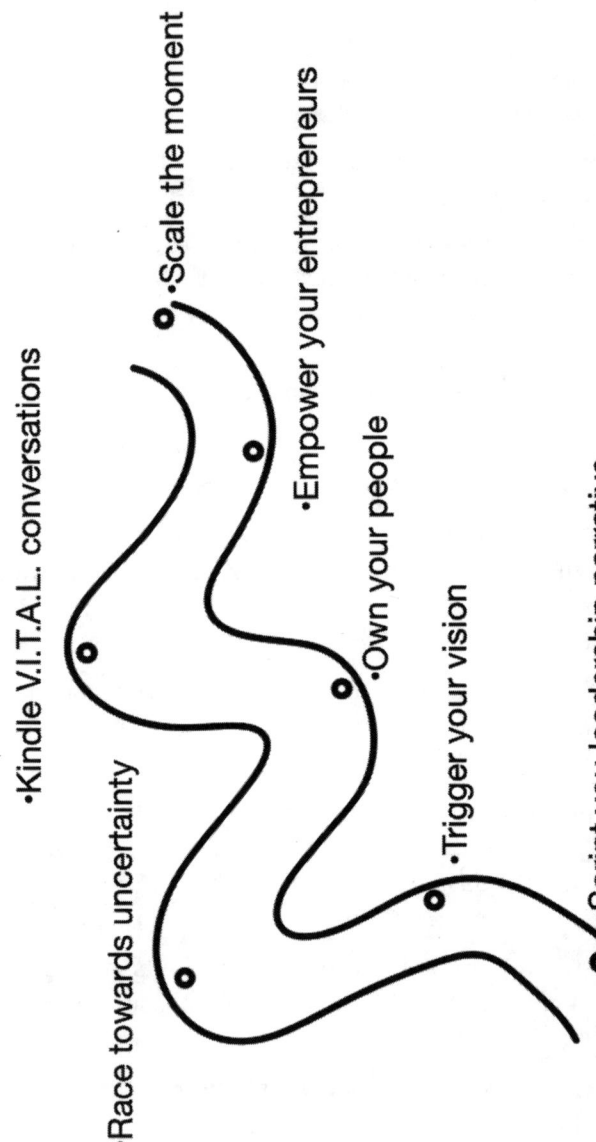

Figure 6.2: *STROKES: The Map of Leadership*

- Race towards uncertainty
- Kindle V.I.T.A.L. conversations
- Scale the moment
- Empower your entrepreneurs
- Own your people
- Trigger your vision
- Script you leadership narrative

'A story is a chain link of events and their cause and effect. A narrative, however, focuses on the way the story is told. The experiences, biases and perspectives of the narrator make the story into a narrative.

'The sun rising on the beach is an event—the sheer magic of the rays unfurling in various hues forming beautiful pictures mingled with the clouds. The flurry of human activity signalling hope and hard work and the nostalgic memories of idyllic days playing on the beach as children is a narrative.

'Your resume is the bare story of your skills and achievements. Your leadership narrative is the representation of your leadership DNA. It draws on your passion and values and paints the picture of how you live them in reality.

'How does narrative, more specifically scripting your leadership narrative make you a better leader?

'Archana loves dogs. As a child, she would play with all the dogs in her neighbourhood, stray ones, pets, every dog. Finally, when she was ten her parents got her a golden retriever of her own. From then on, Archana's journey always had a companion. Growing up Archana dabbled with different jobs but was unhappy being the cubicle dweller.

'It was at this stage that she came in for mentoring and began scripting her leadership narrative.

'The first step in scripting a powerful leadership narrative is to seek and answer your calling.

'The one place the doorkeepers cannot enter is your core. Your purpose that drives you. You can call it you're calling. Calling creates passion. Author and educator Stephen Covey calls it "finding your own voice." It is finding purpose, meaning and fulfilment in your life. It means understanding yourself, your passion and your destiny.

'Michael Novak, in his bestselling book *Business as a Calling*, describes four characteristics of a calling [5]:

- A calling is unique to you. You find yourself. It is self-knowledge, self-identity and self-fulfilment.

- A calling requires talent. According to Logan Pearsall Smith, "The test of a vocation is the love of the drudgery it involves."

- A calling reveals its presence by the enjoyment and renewed energies we get when we practise our craft.

- A calling is not easy to uncover. But when you find it, it drives you and your desire to achieve greatness.

'For Archana, this was a simple step. She was a dog lover and loved all aspects of her life that revolved around the canines. In her first draft she had written, "my calling is to be with animals, to help them live in human-dominant places better. I want to create deeper relation between man and dog."

'Triggering your calling is the first chapter in your leadership narrative. Like all great stories that have stayed in our hearts and memories, the next step in the leadership narrative script is defining the dragons.'

DRAGONS AND THE DEEP BLUE SEA

'Dragons represent the fiery, fire-breathing opponents you have in your narrative. Archana's biggest dragon was that she had no idea how her passion will pay enough for her to leave the job. She knew she did not belong in the tall buildings, glass-covered and sterile.

'She wanted to run in the park and cuddle her pets. Yet her calling would not pay. Archana's dragon essentially was the ambit of her ambition.

'As a leader, while you script your leadership narrative, it is important to consider what boundaries we draw for ourselves. This is our deep blue sea. As a leader what do you seek to change, disrupt, create or preserve? How much of this ambition do you bring to your leadership?

'What is the solid ground that you stand and how do you plan to navigate the deep blue sea?

'Another concern in the ambit of ambition is how wide should you cast your net? Defining the boundaries of your ambition clearly gives you a clear playing field and marks all the dragons.

'While working on her script, Archana found that she had boundaried her ambitions to being with her dogs. However, while scripting about the dragons that need to be slayed, she passionately wrote about how to care for the canines, how certain foods were better and what does a new pup require. As she wrote her narrative, it was clear she was looking at the dragons but Archana also had her own personal army and she did not recognize it.'

CREATING YOUR ARMY

'What is the narrative you are not telling? Are you interweaving personal ambition and talents to organizational or social growth?

'When looking at the real-life stories of Mahatma Gandhi, Lincoln or Mandela, we see what it means to embody this kind of awareness and congruence in interweaving personal and organizational and social goals.

'Archana lacked this congruence. This is where a leadership narrative is more than self-awareness. The "know thyself" needs to be married to bring change in others.

'How could Archana bring change in others?

'Archana's army would consist of all those thoughts, values and actions that she believes would find congruence in leading other minds to bring change.

'Remember Mahatma Gandhi had his personal belief in truth and nonviolence and he lead his countrymen towards independence by showing them how the future could change.

'In Archana's narrative, she scripted her army to be her ability to initiate a smoother journey for new pet owners. She had both the passion and the competence to do it.

'In this stage, Archana concentrated on understanding how she could leverage her passion into changing and creating better experiences for others.

'Of course, the actual battle is in the open market, out there in the midst of competition, chaos and leading minds that have not yet grasped this narrative.'

END GAME AND TRANSFORMATION

'Most leadership narratives define their passion and the dragons. Fewer deliver. One reason is they do not complete the narrative. A story is incomplete till you end with "and they lived happily ever after."

'Ending your leadership narrative at building your army means you feel you are ready for battle but that is only in your imagination.

'The end game will be to narrate what will happen in reality. It can be argued that in a way predicting and forecasting the real battle is also preparing the army. But there is a difference. In *The Art of War* Sun Tsu (6) shares,

> If you know the enemy and know yourself, you need not fear the result of a hundred battles. If you know yourself but not the enemy, for every victory gained you will also suffer a defeat. If you know neither the enemy nor yourself, you will succumb in every battle.

'How does the battle narrative draft looks like?

'For Archana, it meant prioritizing her battle strategies. Her first step was to understand her potential customers, figure out their wants, their resistances and work out strategies that will be easy to win.

'She knew she had a lot of knowledge that new pet owners may require. But it would be impractical to go around the world teaching them as the lone battle strategy. That option also did not slay her dragon of creating a profitable business.

'Digging deeper, she found out that new dog owners also required help buying all dog products.

'Archana's narrative now leads her to curate smooth transition for both man and dog for new pet owners. She created a great product—a man and dog kit that had all the things new dog owners might require. The highlight was it included a comprehensive manual, details about nearby vets, schedules to keep in mind and a week of intervention from a dog trainer.

'Archana's passion became the one-stop shop for all new dog owners and she lead them in their journey with passion, love and deep knowledge about dogs.

'Rewriting her leadership narrative from a miserable cubicle dweller, who had snatches of free time to walk her dog, Archana now owns a profitable business creating smother transitions for new pet owners.

'Scripting a powerful leadership narrative gives you a point of reference and gives you perspective on the kind of leader you are and can become.

'As the leadership guru, Warren Bennis reminds us, "The process of becoming a leader is much the same as the process of becoming an integrated human being. This process begins and ends with the stories of our lives."'

ARJUN'S DIARY: MY LEADERSHIP MASTERSTROKE

- How do we keep the doorkeepers of inertia away?
- What is my biggest inertia?
- How does narrative, more specifically, scripting your leadership narrative will make me a better leader?
- What do I want to change, disrupt, create and preserve?
- Who are my dragons?
- What does my army look like?

- What is the final future reality that my battle would win?

- What is my draft leadership narrative?

NOTES AND REFERENCES

1. Bryant J. Roger Bannister showed us how to combine sport and everyday living. The Guardian. 2014 May. Available from: https://www.theguardian.com/commentisfree/2014/may/05/roger-bannister-four-minute-mile-combine-sport-living

2. Hooper W, Rawls MK. Borders Group, Inc.'s final chapter: How a bookstore giant failed in the digital age. Chapter 11 Bankruptcy Case Studies. 2014. Available from: http://trace.tennessee.edu/utk_studlawbankruptcy/38

3. Winning stroke: Interview with Mr. Maulik Desai, Head, Crossword Bookstores. Business World People. Available from: http://bwpeople.businessworld.in/article/Winning-Stroke-Interview-with-Mr-Maulik-Desai-Head-Crossword-Bookstores-/20-06-2018-152346/

4. Robin Sharma quotes. Available from: www.brainyquote.com

5. Novak M, Novak J. Business as a calling. Free Press. 2013

6. *Art of war* quotes. Available from: www.goodreads.com https://suntzusaid.com/book/3/18

TRIGGER YOUR PURPOSE

Arjun and Ved moved back to their terrace table for breakfast. Looking at the vast ocean in front of them Ved asked, 'What do you see beyond the horizon?'

Arjun looked the ocean for some time and said, 'We don't see beyond the ocean. We know the horizon is an illusion and once we get there, there will be another horizon farther down, keeping in mind the earth is spherical.'

'You have precisely defined the concept of "illusion of knowledge." Knowledge has its limitations. Daniel Boorstin wrote what Stephen Hawking later popularized, "The greatest enemy of knowledge is not ignorance, but the illusion of knowledge." Take, for example, a carpenter. He has to produce fine quality furniture. He has a set of tools with him. He works with only these tools as he was taught to work with them. He knows he needs a hammer to push the nail into the wall, but he does not explore the other end of the hammer that can help him pull out the nail. He works inside the horizon of his knowledge. In such cases, the person works from what he knows, codifies his knowledge to prescriptions to be used in need. Not just individuals, teams, organizations and generations of humanity often work inside the horizon from their illusionary knowledge base.

'The problems arise when what you know is no longer relevant or the external conditions change fast. Knowledge provides the allure of comfort and many organizations and cultures never rose out of its depth. The invasion of Rome and Greece, the multiple invasions from the Mongols, Mughals and later the East India Company in India, the death of the Auto Industry in Detroit, the invisible slow annihilation of human connectivity in the digital world are all the result of looking only inside of the horizon.

'Like you said, you cannot actually see beyond the horizon. Not with human eyes. But our minds, our spirit can recognize the vast possibilities. Thinking beyond the horizon is what leaders should do. Warren Bennis calls this the horizon thinking [1]. A future focus that transcends the prescribed and commonly accepted corporate goals and instead focuses on the future by forming a shared vision with the leader's inner vision and the follower's vision of its possibilities. The thrill of the possibilities beyond, the call to adventure of the unknown and the drive to meet them make leaders who create disruption.'

'I understand what you are saying Ved. The calling that brings us out of the casino is the vision of the leader. The problem is when we read, learn and talk about such calling, the examples are Steve Jobs and how he had the vision of breaking the monopoly of giants or the touchscreen technology and visionaries that are few and far in the course of history. I would like to believe that the vision is something that all of us can work towards with introspection and discussions and some elbow grease. It is very important for me to understand this as today the organization stands democratized and everyone wants to lead. But the process looks overwhelming for many. How can I, as a leader, develop this vision?'

BUDDHA VS RAMA

'The key question to discovering the vision in you is to answer "What is it that you really want to do?" As Malvolio reads in his letter in the Shakespearean play *Twelfth Night* [2], "Some are born great, some achieve greatness and some have greatness thrust upon them." The concept of being a leader with a greater vision is actually having a greater sense of your personal sense of gravity. Let us see further.

'Krishna in Mahabharata was a born leader. The stories of his greatness can be seen from his battles even as a baby. He is probably one of the very few examples of the "people born great" part of the quote. But for many, greatness is achieved. Compare the same to Buddha. As Prince Siddhartha, he saw the plight of the old, poor and hurt people and wanted to know how to move beyond the pain of belonging. His was a long inner journey that led him to enlightenment. It is the same for Mozart, Einstein, Tiger Woods, Sachin Tendulkar and Shakespeare himself. In fact, as you mentioned Steve Jobs, he is also one of those leaders who achieved greatness. In his iconic speech at Stanford in 2005, he recites his experience in three stories' [3]:

> The first story is about connecting the dots. I dropped out of Reed College after the first 6 months, but then stayed around as a drop-in for another 18 months or so before I really quit.... And 17 years later I did go to college. After six months, I couldn't see the value in it. I had no idea what I wanted to do with my life and no idea how college was going to help me figure it out. Because I had dropped out and didn't have to take the normal classes, I decided to take a calligraphy class. I learned about serif and sans serif typefaces, about varying the amount of space between different letter combinations, about what makes great typography great. It was beautiful, historical, artistically subtle in a way that science can't capture, and I found it fascinating.... None of this had even a hope of any practical application in my life. But 10 years later, when we were designing the first Macintosh computer, it all came back to me. And we designed it all into the Mac.... If I had never dropped out, I would have never dropped in on this calligraphy class, and personal computers might not have the wonderful typography that they do....
>
> My second story is about love and loss.
>
> I was lucky—I found what I loved to do early in life. Woz and I started Apple in my parents' garage when I was 20. We worked hard, and in 10 years, Apple had grown from just the two of us in a garage into a $2 billion company with over 4,000 employees. We had just released our finest creation—the Macintosh—a year earlier, and I had just turned 30. And then I got fired.... I didn't see it then, but it turned out that getting fired from Apple was the best thing that could have ever happened to me. The heaviness of being successful was replaced by the lightness of being a

beginner again, less sure about everything. It freed me to enter one of the most creative periods of my life.

During the next five years, I started a company named NeXT; another company named Pixar, and fell in love with an amazing woman who would become my wife. Pixar went on to create the world's first computer animated feature film, Toy Story, and is now the most successful animation studio in the world. In a remarkable turn of events, Apple bought NeXT, I returned to Apple, and the technology we developed at NeXT is at the heart of Apple's current renaissance…. Your work is going to fill a large part of your life, and the only way to be truly satisfied is to do what you believe is great work. And the only way to do great work is to love what you do. If you haven't found it yet, keep looking. Don't settle….

My third story is about death.

When I was 17, I read a quote that went something like: 'If you live each day as if it was your last, someday you'll most certainly be right.' It made an impression on me, and since then, for the past 33 years, I have looked in the mirror every morning and asked myself: 'If today were the last day of my life, would I want to do what I am about to do today?' And whenever the answer has been 'No' for too many days in a row, I know I need to change something….

'And the last place, to have greatness thrust on you is the way most people have faced it. Lord Rama was all set out to become the king when he was exiled for 14 years. He accepted the situation and lived the turnaround life as an ascetic with dedication [4]. Alexander the Great [5], much to our thinking of a hero born great, had it thrust upon him. Succeeding his father at the age of 20, Alexander went on an unprecedented military campaign to create the largest kingdom in ancient world history. These are people who rose up to the crisis and circumstance made them great. Did Winston Churchill achieve greatness, or did the Second World War present him with a crisis in which he was able to rise to the occasion?

'Not to forget the man who began the micro finance movement of which your organization is also a part—Muhammad Yunus, the Bangladeshi economist, Nobel Prize winner and the founder of Grameen Bank [6]. The famine that hit Bangladesh in 1974 pushed him to do something about poverty. During his visits to the poorest households in the village of *Jobra*, he realized that a small loan can make a big difference to a poor person. He made his first loan to 42 women in the village, with just USD $27 from his own pocket. With this money, the women were able to make baskets, sell them and quickly repay the money they borrowed from him. He began to see that small loans would not only help them survive, but create in them the spark of enterprise and this could empower them and pull them out of poverty. This small investment had astounding and unexpected ripple effects. Indeed, it was the impetus for what eventually led to the global micro finance movement.

'Discovering the leadership vision is not a gift you are born with but a badge that you acquire after a lot of work. It is rather unrealistic to think that you can develop beyond the horizon vision and a leader mindset overnight.'

YOUR LEADERSHIP VISION

'The first step in discovering your leadership vision is to have a better understanding of the leader you are. Think about the following questions:

1. How often are you a leader in your role?

2. How have you addressed the changing market relationships with your customers?

3. How have you owned your people? Been the Pied Piper?

4. How are you rising to the challenges of technology, economy and global crisis?

5. What opportunities in leadership do these contextual challenges present to you?

'Your leadership vision is an expression of what you want to do in your role as a leader.

'Your leadership vision is separate from your personal vision in life and also from your organizational vision.

'Consider Mahatma Gandhi—his personal life vision to strive towards a life of good and a life in moderation with truth, honesty and non-violence as its pillars. He was a value-based leader who wanted India (organizational vision) to be free of the colonial rule. In a country of farmers that has never invaded any other country in its history, a military vision would have only led to bloodshed. Gandhi saw the reason the British came to India were our resources and matched it to our countries greatest strengths in resilience. His leadership vision of non-violence and non-cooperation inspires the world leaders a 150 years after his death.

'While you explore your leadership vision, keep these points in mind.'

1. **It is yours what you want to do. It reflects your personal values. Own it.**

   'Psychiatrist Carl Jung said, "Your vision will become clear only when you look into your heart. Who looks outside dreams, who looks inside awakens" [7]. While formulating your vision, it is important to start from the inside as the outside world can dilute and distract you from your passion. A vision that comes from within is authentic and owned. When you try to follow someone, both the pride of ownership and the freedom of choice are missing. A vision formulated this way will be too weak to overcome obstacles from the environment.

   'In the words of Aristotle, "Where our talents and the needs of the world cross, there lies our vocation" [8]. Your leadership vision should match who you are. A pre-requirement, therefore, would be to become self-aware. A leadership vision created with awareness provides clarity.

   'Ask yourself what do you bring to your leadership vision. And also ask what gets in your way.

'Leadership traits, competencies and weakness form who you are, and the current generation of employees looks for these nine competencies:

a. Shared vision

b. Conversations

c. Adaptive resilience

d. Collaboration

e. Comfort in chaos

f. Tech-savvy

g. Self-leadership

h. Global connectedness

i. Learning agility

'For each of these traits think about how you have actioned it. Many of these competencies are interrelated and blend into each other.

'While looking at your leadership, look for resonance. Maybe you resonate a lot with being tech-savvy and blend learning agility and resilience well.

'While your vision will always be sparked by your passion, it is important to be aware of what will get in your way. A clear understanding of both your strength and weakness will ensure your vision is beyond the horizon but not lost in the stars.'

2. **Your vision should have space for evolution as you and your ideas grow.**

'Your leadership vision should have space for expansion and evolution. It is important to know what you believe in, what is your North Star and what can be changed. Connecting your leadership vision to a transforming process of becoming the best leader, you can be is a continuous process of evolution. As you look at your vision, check yourself:

- Are you committed to transformation? As business continues to move at unprecedented speed, can your vision shift paradigms and expand to new ones?

- Do you recognize the interconnectedness of your vision with your people? Today, people want equal ownership of your vision. Does your vision encapsulate the opportunity to maximize potential, profits and people?

- Does your vision hold the space for expansion? Like Goldsmith says "What got you here won't get you there," your vision should have space to deliberately enter into "beginner's mind" when facing new challenges. Do you seek to continuously expand your consciousness?

- Is your leadership vision circular? In the way post-industrial revolution linear economies are giving way to a circular sustainable economy, leadership vision in the present turbulent times needs to be circular—an iterative process to plan–act–listen for reaction–iterate.'

3. **Your vision is larger than you.**

'Your vision should contribute to the success of your team, your organization and your country.

'While the vision is yours, it is not about you. John Maxwell, in his book *Intentional Living* [9], talks about the significance of living beyond yourself. It is the same with leadership vision. Does your vision cater to Maxwell's five significance?

- Giving beyond yourself,

- Serving beyond yourself,

- Thinking beyond yourself,

- Loving beyond yourself, and

- Seeing beyond yourself.

'The purpose of having a vision beyond yourself is best told in this parable of the power of purpose. The story of three bricklayers is a multi-faceted parable with many different variations but is rooted in an authentic story. After the great fire of 1666 that levelled London, the world's most famous architect, Christopher Wren, was commissioned to rebuild St Paul's Cathedral [10].'

One day in 1671, Christopher Wren observed three bricklayers on a scaffold, one crouched, one half-standing and one standing tall, working very hard and fast. To the first bricklayer, Christopher Wren asked the question, 'What are you doing?' to which the bricklayer replied, 'I'm a bricklayer. I'm working hard laying bricks to feed my family.' The second bricklayer, responded, 'I'm a builder. I'm building a wall.' But the third bricklayer, the most productive of the three and the future leader of the group, when asked the question, 'What are you doing?' replied with a gleam in his eye, 'I'm a cathedral builder. I'm building a great cathedral to The Almighty.'

'Victor Frankel made this clear in his book, *The Meaning of Life* [11]. He wrote about how some people survived the holocaust, but so many didn't. One of the things he identified was those who had a purpose or reason to continue to live that was beyond themselves tended to survive, while those who were focused primarily on themselves did not. Those who survived found some meaning in their painful circumstances. The meaning they found was in caring for and helping others in this horrible experience.'

UNLEASH THE LEADER IN YOU

'How do you lead in a way that reflects the authentic you and not a mere shadow of someone else?

'It is rather easy and many times, it is expected of you to follow the footsteps of someone. This can be because you admire the person or it is a role expectation. Slowly, you tend to adopt the persona of the person you follow. It can also be an expectation of how a leader is supposed to be—expert in his skills, TED Talk like presence, the casual informality and humility filled authority.

'At the same time, being authentic does not mean saying anything you feel like. Your leadership vision should help you move from impulse to insight. The idea is to show up as a whole person, one that cares about others, is inclusive and yet has space for individuality.

Arjun was furiously scribbling a lot of thoughts that bubbled inside him as Ved explained the nuances of leadership vision. He at once knew his first flaw. He had made his organizational vision as his vision. In reality there is more to a company than its leader and more to a leader than his company. By forcibly trying to merge the two, Arjun had in fact diluted his vision. He now wanted to explore what being this whole person and having an authentic vision looked like. He wanted to write his vision to.

'Ved, how do I write such a vision?'

'While I cannot tell you how to exactly word your vision, I can guide you to the path.' They had moved from the terrace back to the Vetaal's haunt and over tall glasses of fresh juices; Ved continued, 'It is called a vision. So start by looking. Look around you, within you. Listen deeply with all your senses. This process is called 360 vision.'

LOOK WITHIN YOU

'The first place to look will be within you. Close your eyes and take a deep breath. Slowly become comfortable in your place. Now imagine walking down a flight of stairs. You are slowly moving to the basement and lower. The stairs open into your secret paradise. Imagine this place. This is your place. How does it look? What do you see?

'Notice this place. Listen to it.

'Listen, notice and accept everything that is there. They are all a part of what you want. Your passion, your calling, your fears even.

Figure 7.1: *360° Vision*

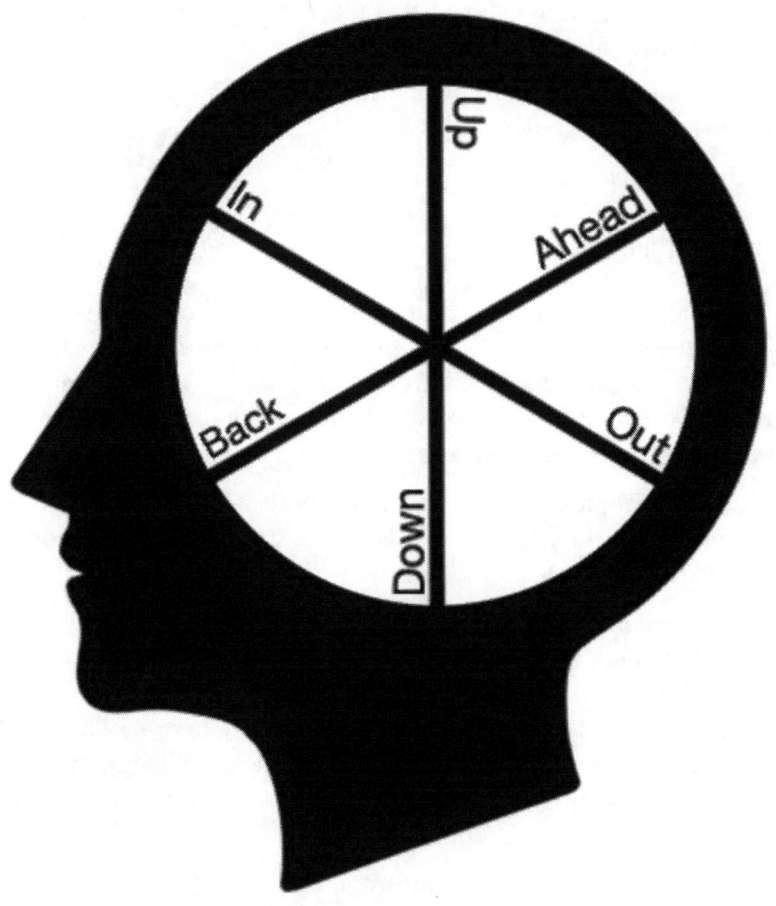

'Now walk slowly into your paradise and sit down in a place of your choice in your secret paradise. And listen. Just listen. Listen to your feelings. How do you feel? Listen to your passion. What draws you? Listen to your fears. What is keeping you chained?

'Consider answering the question, what is my passion? How do I want it to become my vision? Once you are comfortable in your answers, slowly move out of this place. Climb back those stairs and slowly open your eyes.'

Arjun had a sense of calm when he opened his eyes. He quickly wrote down his thoughts.

Ved continued.

LOOK OUTSIDE

'Now take a deep breath and look around you. Imagine your entire world, with all that means to you, is around you. This is your playing ground. What do you want to do? How do you want to make a difference in others' lives? Who are these others? Listen to your heart as you open yourself to leading beyond yourself.

'Listen to people and their needs. Find out how your vision can shape their future. Like Ernest Hemingway said, "When people talk, listen completely."

'Many leaders were born and became great visionaries because they had their ear to the ground. A complete turnaround of a leadership vision after looking outside is the story of Ashoka the Great—the last Mauryan king who ruled India between 273 and 232 BC. After the bloody Kalinga War, he was so deeply moved and pained by the suffering that he denounced his throne and all his wealth and adopted Buddhism [12].

'As the pioneering cultural anthropologist, Margaret Mead says, "Never doubt that a small group of thoughtful, concerned citizens can change the world. Indeed it is the only thing that ever has."

'Now it is your turn. Look around you to see how can you make a difference.'

LOOK BEHIND

'There was never a path, only your footprint. As you walked, you made the path, like a ship's wake.

'Look behind you to see those footprints, like the ship's wake; it's a reminder that for every journey there is a departure and clear log of our experiences. Wise navigators always look into the ship's wake, read the logs to understand their next cruise better.

'Looking back gives us the lessons learnt in past experiences, allows us the advantage of hindsight to move ahead.

'Have you ever wondered how all the business giants struck gold with college garage projects, investors who always bought the right stocks or how an entrepreneur hit it big time? Most of them had a theory for speculation—a promise of possibilities. Being a great leader is also about intuiting possibilities. Intuition is your unconscious brain working on the big data of your experience to show you the way.

'Look behind, listen to your intuition, appreciate your lessons and carry your experiences.'

LOOK AHEAD

'Are you looking at today's needs...or tomorrow's possibilities? The very idea of a vision is your ability to look beyond the horizon.

'John R. Childress, author of *Leverage: The CEO's Guide to Corporate Culture* [13] compares the beyond the horizon visions of the two CEOs of Microsoft, Gates and Ballmer. Way back in 1995, Microsoft was booming. When most CEOs would keep with the proven winning formula, Bill Gates saw beyond the horizon to the future rise of Internet. And on May 26, 1995, issued the historical internal memo—the Internet tidal wave. The basic message was "We were wrong about the Internet and we are going to do a 90° turn and go full steam to dominate the Internet." As a result they crushed NetScape and Sun and completely took over the web browser market.

'Fast-forward in the life cycle of once dominant Microsoft and there is another story to be told, one of a different leadership focus and different results. Today, just 10 years after crushing NetScape and Sun and completely dominating the web browser market, Microsoft is a distant second place to Google Chrome. Steve Ballmer, former CEO of Microsoft for the years during the "browser wars" and up until just recently, had a very different leadership style than Bill Gates. He ran Microsoft from quarterly results to quarterly results, not for the long term. It's amazing how difficult it is to think about the future and see the "over the horizon" stuff when your day is full with "busyness."

'When Satya Nadella made his first public appearance as the new CEO of Microsoft in 2014, he did something very unusual for a leader of the software giant.

'He made a pronouncement on day 1—"The world is about cloud-first, mobile-first [14]," and never once mentioned the word Windows. Since that point, Nadella has delivered. Microsoft has emerged as a major vendor of cloud computing services, especially for big businesses, challenging Amazon Web Services in the rapidly growing cloud infrastructure market.

'As a leader, look ahead, look beyond the horizon and look at the possibilities in tomorrow.'

LOOK UP

'If I have seen further it is by standing on the shoulders of giants— Sir Isaac Newton wrote these lines in his letter to Robert Hooke in 1696 [15].

'Newton, however, got this saying from George Herbert who wrote in 1651: "A dwarf on a giant's shoulders sees farther of the two."

'In 1621, Robert Burton's recorded to have written "A dwarf standing on the shoulders of a giant may see farther than a giant himself."

'Dating the lines even backward,

'In 1159, John of Salisbury said: "We are like dwarfs on the shoulders of giants, so that we can see more than they."

'Finally, the thread ends in the words of Bernard of Chartres in 1130, "We are like dwarfs standing upon the shoulders of giants, and so able to see more and see farther than the ancients."

'As the quote itself and its thread show us, we are always a product of the wisdom handed down to us. Leaders need to know when to tap into the wisdom of the past and when the collective whole of the team would win. In the words of Diogenes of Sinope, "Wise leaders generally have wise counsellors because it takes a wise person themselves to distinguish them."

'Look at the progress of the analogue leaders to lead effectively in the digital age. Who and what inspires your vision?'

LOOK DOWN

'"The function of leadership is to produce more leaders, not more followers." The quote was of Ralph Nader, but the CEO of HCL Vineet Nayar lives this kind of vision [16].

'How would it be for the leader to learn from his followers and to hand over the keys and step aside? How empowering would the youngsters find to be accountable for their actions? Vineet Nayar writing about his policies of employee first, customer second in an HBR article [17] mentions',

And here's another audacious idea: Management could be held accountable in that inverted role. At HCL we launched a super-360-degree appraisal, in which any employee can assess a manager who has an impact on his or her work. What's more, the appraisals of every senior manager, including me, were published on the intranet and viewable by all 87,000 employees.

In most businesses, true value is created in what I call the 'value zone', where employees work directly with customers to solve their problems. My advice: Don't wait to see high engagement levels before letting young employees enter this zone. Unleash their abilities, and then step aside.

'Look and notice,

'What you can learn from your followers?

'How can you empower them?

'How can your vision help create more leaders for tomorrow?'

WRITE YOUR LEADERSHIP VISION

A 360 visioning gives you a holistic picture of your leadership situation. Now that you have that image of what you will accomplish, write a brief story about your leadership vision.

1. Include your experience, address the future and make it empowering for your followers.

2. Make it a compelling story of what you went through to accomplish each of the results for the questions you answered. Make it about you; what moves you and what will compel your followers to move.

3. Create an image of the future you see. It should stretch beyond the horizon but should be achievable on stretching.

4. Now write your vision down so that your team feels empowered to follow.

REFERENCES

1. Bennis W. On becoming a leader. New York, NY: Perseus Books Group; 2009.

MASTERSTROKES

2. Shakespeare W. Twelfth night.

3. Jobs S. Text of Steve Jobs' commencement address at Stanford. 2005. Available from: https://news.stanford.edu/2005/06/14/jobs-061505/

4. *Ramayana.* An Indian epic written by Valmiki.

5. Alexander the Great. Wikipedia. Available from: https://en.wikipedia.org/wiki/Alexander_the_Great

6. What is Grameen Bank and who is Muhammad Yunus? Milaap. Available from: https://milaap.org/stories/what-is-grameen-bank-and-who-is-muhammad-yunus

7. Carl Jung quotes. Available from: https://www.quotes.net/quote/14623

8. Aristotle quotes. Available from: https://www.goodreads.com/quotes/431261-where-your-talents-and-the-needs-of-the-world-cross

9. Maxwell J. Intentional living: Choosing a life that matters. New York, NY: Center Street; 2015.

10. The story of three bricklayers—A parable about the power of purpose. 2019. Available from: https://sacredstructures.org/mission/the-story-of-three-bricklayers-a-parable-about-the-power-of-purpose/

11. Frankl V. Man's search for meaning: The classic tribute to hope from the Holocaust. London: Rider; 2008.

12. Ashoka. Available from: https://www.newworldencyclopedia.org/entry/ashoka

13. Gates vs. Balmer. Available from: https://blog.johnrchildress.com/2014/07/03/seeing-beyond-the-horizon-and-strategic-leadership/

14. How Microsoft bounced back. CNBC Tech. 2018 Dec. Available from: https://www.cnbc.com/2018/12/03/microsoft-recovery-how-satya-nadella-did-it.html

15. Moving words, Sir Isaac Newton [online]. Available from: https://www.bbc.co.uk/worldservice/learningenglish/movingwords/shortlist/newton.shtml

16. Ralph Nader quotes. Available from: https://www.brainyquote.com/quotes/ralph_nader_110188

17. Nayar V. Put your employees first. Harv Bus Rev. 2010 Jul.

8   RACE TOWARDS UNCERTAINTY

Arjun wrote his first draft of a 360 vision and looked forward to the next steps. In the evening they sat down again to another discussion and the next step in the Masterstrokes Leadership Journey.

The clouds suddenly cast long shadows turning the coastal town into a gloomy cold place. It was not raining yet, although the tide had risen to levels dangerous for swimming.

Arjun and Ved decided to stay on at the beach for a while longer. Watching the high tide and the waves turning ferocious, Arjun began,

'Writing my 360 vision has opened a lot of thoughts inside me. The road ahead earlier meant a flat road with a few roadblocks, rough roads and bends. I could still see my way and was fairly confident of the journey. Now this path is like dune bashing on a desert. No roads, the dunes keep changing and if you go too deep without having an idea, you may be lost admits the sands. The signboard, "Caution: Uncertainty Ahead" is everywhere.

'As I analyse both my vision and the way my organization MOOLA is growing, I am stuck with two questions.

'The market has seen a decently steady growth in the peer-to-peer lending space and at Moola, we worked our systems and strategies to meet the market. Overnight in 2017, the mandate for a license came in and we scrambled to meet the requirements. It was a great initiative I agree, but the ground level work changed. Later demonetization was announced. Ideally speaking it set off a good turn for us. While we were not the first ones in the industry, we managed to harness that change in our favour and created a larger base of lenders and borrowers. Of course, it would have been great to look for lenders with deep pockets but we have the RBI cap of lending to maximum ₹10 lakhs. This made lenders with serious money lose interest in the process. This is how the field works and we decided to increase the base. So we looked for lenders and borrowers with even very small amounts in transaction. Early this year, the 10-lakh-mandate was lifted to 50 lakhs. We are reworking on the changes but the world is hit with the pandemic.

'How do we foresee such changes and how do we defend ourselves from the attacks out of the blue?

'How can I lead my people and my company when the changes are so unpredictable and fast?'

'The second question that I am thinking about covers a lot more ground. Even before I started Moola, in college, we learnt everything has a life and everything has a price. By that logic, death is the biggest leveller in all games. *Yama* is after all called the *Dharmaraja* for this reason.

'Apparently he rides his buffalo and walks towards us all at a steady pace and the distance between the noose in his hand and us is time we have on Earth. Taking the same allegory to my products, all products have to die. The wagon wheels gave up to the automobiles, the long letters written in ink and posted at the local post office died carrying the romanticism of long afternoons writing to loved ones to emails and shorter text messages.

'As a leader how do I predict the distance between the noose and my strategy or product?'

THE ANATOMY OF UNCERTAINTY

Ved wanted to talk about this aspect in the session today and was overjoyed when Arjun brought out the questions himself. A different orbit of progress happens when the learner and mentor align in their thoughts.

Figure 8.1: *The Anatomy of Uncertainty*

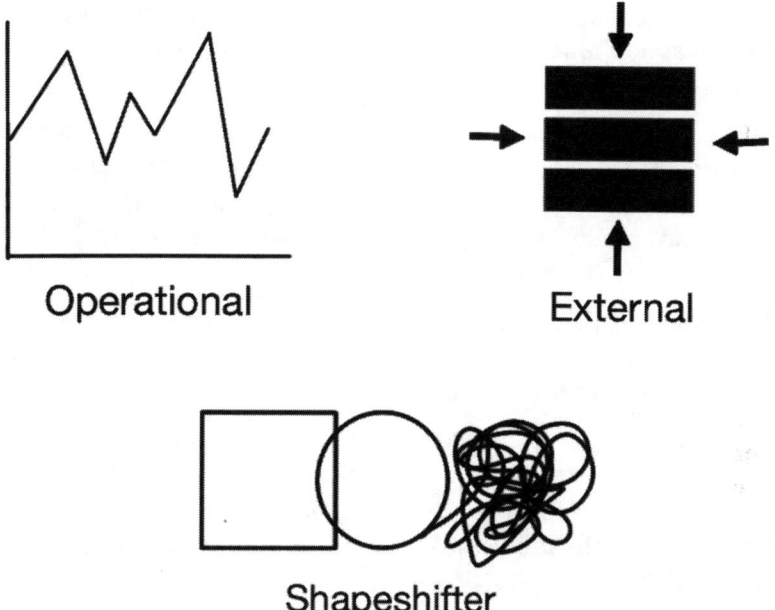

Operational

External

Shapeshifter

Ved answered, 'Right on the heels of the financial recession in 2008, Steven Covey released his book, Predictable Results in Unpredictable Times in 2009 [1]. One quote that stayed with me all these years is, "no leader can compute all the uncertainties of the future into a set of certainties."

'To add on, in the last decade since the recession, the pace, scale and the ferocious impact of the uncertainties have only grown. To control or even mitigate uncertainties, we first need to understand it.

'The changes and uncertainties in the economy can hurt you, but your inability to respond to them will hurt you more.

'The anatomy of uncertainty is much like the turtles. We always think that the turtle is a soft, small animal that lives inside the hideous dome shell. But the truth is the shell is the turtle. Its bones go around the shell and are part of the turtle. In much the same way, while the uncertainty looks like a separate shell, it is built into the skeletal system of our business.

'Uncertainties can be of the operational kind. This is the garden variety, vanilla uncertainty like the shifts in demand and distribution or a slow growth towards a new product or service.

'And then there are the external uncertainties like the geopolitical conflicts, global economic conditions, pandemics and global warming. While we don't have much control here, many can be waited out or the problem is large enough for us to gather forces and ride the tide.

'What is new today is the shape shifter variety of uncertainty. I name it shape shifter as they hit you out of the blue and shift the existing shape and structure of your business.

'Let me tell you the story of Murugan who manufactures umbrellas. He has a small manufacturing unit outside the city. His city has clear monsoon rains, a few spells in October and blistering heat in April and May.

'His operational uncertainty was the climatic demand for his product. He knew people bought umbrellas only after the first rain of monsoon. In the last 15 years, he had also seen an increase in umbrella sales during summer. Global warming, rising temperature and the advertisements of harmful effects of sun radiation kept this business driving in summer.

'Two years back, a large theme park with jungle theme and farm themes and a mall opened in his city. People flocked to these places especially in the summer school holidays. The crowd surprisingly did not mind the rains as many areas had awnings and shaded walkways.

'Murugan saw this as an opportunity and next year began to manufacture more. The first year as he expected he made a sizeable amount in profits due to the increase in sales. He decided to repeat the next year.

[And that is when the shape shifter hit. The theme park and the mall decided to offer free ponchos to all customers and absorbed this in their entry fee. The advertisements to the same hit all channels, crowds of delighted customers came to the theme parks, the rains came on time but Murugan's umbrellas went unsold.

'For businesses that are unprepared, these massive changes come in without warning obscuring future growth.

'Another reason I call this shape shifter is because the change can come from anywhere. It is common to site examples of how Apple's iPhone killed Nokia or how Amazon has wiped out the bookstores. These uncertainties don't just belong to the big companies with large pockets to spend.

'Let us look at the biggest crowd in India—the youngsters and children. Throughout their life, students in India are on a race towards greater marks. This is mainly because we have only a few good schools and colleges and too many bright minds. So the bright minds work really hard to get inside the portals of the bigger colleges in engineering, medicine, pass CA, etc. The system of schools, colleges, private education institutions that help in the entrance tests work the students for the top grades. It is very hard work and the competition is high.

'These are the known uncertainties in this field—the rising competition, more players, more students, changing syllabi or exam pattern. And then comes Amol Bhave, from Jabalpur [2].

'The 17-year-old in 2013 decided to learn from the Massive Open Online Courses (MOOCs) and enrolled himself to courses from MIT on edX. After watching many OpenCourseWare (OCW) lectures and taking courses through MITx—including 6.002x (Circuits and Electronics), Bhave organized and started his own online course, named 6.003z (Signals and Systems), which more than a thousand students took part in. Bhave was one of the early users of OCW and edX. The program—an online learning tool founded by MIT and Harvard University—has emerged as a leader in digital learning innovation, most recently launching the MITx MicroMasters, which enables learners around the world to take online courses toward admission into an MIT master's program. Since MITx launched, more than 70 courses have been accessed by more than 2.5 million learners globally.

'Following the success of 6.003z, Bhave reached out to MIT Professor Anant Agrawal, founder and CEO of edX, thanking him for 6.002x and sharing what that led him to create. Through his success and encouragement, Bhave decided he would try applying to MIT and see what happened. Bhave took the SATs, applied, and after spending many restless nights waiting for the results, received the news of his acceptance and started making plans to move to Massachusetts.

'We are at a turning point of survival and discovery, collectively confronting a moment when the old models of identity are up for grabs, and new models are still forming. Even if we are not aware of any inner need for transformation, our outer world is changing so dramatically that we will not be able to remain as we have been. Today our workplaces are in transition. We are 'reinventing' government.

'Leaders have always shown their mettle in times of liminality. The term comes from Arnold van Gennep, the Belgian anthropologist who first outlined the common patterns in how cultures mark transitions from one human state to another (e.g., from adolescence to adulthood). In his 1909 book, *The Rites of Passage*[3], he described three stages of separation from one world and entry into another. The liminal (or threshold) stage is central. Commenting later on van Gennep's work, anthropologist Victor Turner explained it as "a moment when those being moved in accordance with a cultural script were liberated from normative demands, when they were, indeed, betwixt and between successive lodgements in jural political systems. In this gap between ordered worlds almost anything may happen." Like Margaret Wheatley says, "The things we fear most in organizations—fluctuations, disturbances, imbalances—are the primary sources of creativity."

'We need to celebrate the why not and race towards the rising tide. Leaders need to anticipate change, look not just inside their organization but also outside and peek over the horizon as well.'

ANTICIPATE THE CHANGE

'Arjun let me ask you this. Are the uncertainties really sudden? Even the shape shifter variety? The mandate for license for your industry had been in talks for months before the final announcements came in.

'A few decades ago, a "Kodak moment" meant a picture of happy families, satisfaction and success. Unfortunately, today Eastman Kodak is a case study of how not to ignore the early triggers in the ecosystem [4].

'Kodak's core business was to sell the camera films. Now that all cameras are digital and are part of mobile phones, obviously it is natural for older companies to decline. But Kodak's decline had nothing to do with technology.

'An employee of Kodak created the first prototype of a digital camera in 1975. But they were too myopic to do anything about this new product. Later when they did invest, they stuck to their core competency and created strategies for digital camera on the same lines as film.

'Of course, it can be pointed out that after all nowadays, even digital camera sales are down. Everyone prefers to click on their mobile phones. Again, for Kodak this was not about technology. Much before Facebook even hit the market, Kodak purchased "Ofoto" in 2001. Ofoto was a photo-sharing site. Imagine if they had really developed this business in the way it deserved, Ofoto could have been the Instagram we have today.

'So Kodak pioneered the digital camera and the photo-sharing website. Their technology was future-looking. Their leadership un-fortunately was in the past and Kodak was unable to truly enable the newer business models.

'It is a sad story of lost potential with a lot of lessons.

'The most important lesson being, "How to anticipate the uncertainty?" "How can leaders peek beyond the curve on the road to see what's out there?"'

Arjun added, 'I am reminded of a friend who had a huge collection of songs, was a collector of albums and always had his earplugs on listening to music and yet during a game of Antakshari (a game of tag with songs) he would not remember a single song. Many times as leaders we would have read a trend or has mastered a concept in theory but a myopic vision into our own existing systems creates a bubble many don't come out of.'

'This is true,' agreed Ved.

'The signals of early warning signs to a future disruption are all around us. We just need to look in the right places. I have a list of five places like the Panchabhoota to look for the early signs.'

1. Look at trends

'Like the waves, the trends are very good indicators of the corporate tides. A sudden increase in AI experts is a trend. When such job postings happen from a wide range of industries, suddenly it is an accelerated trend one that is nearing a disruption phase. When more writers entered the market, it created a huge trend to self-publish.

'Train yourself to stand back from your strategies and operational problems and look at the entire ecosystem. Look for changes, anomalies or patterns that don't fit.

'Look at what people are talking on social media. Listen to people on the networking sites of Facebook, Instagram or Twitter. They are the current pulse of the people.'

2. Look at Scalability

'When the Kodak employer came up with the digital camera idea, Kodak did not know how to scale the idea to successful business. A mind-blowing new idea can be in the market already without the knowledge of how to scale. The Segway bikes [5] that are so cool to move around should have become hugely successful. The problem being no one knew how to scale it to real life. For Segway, the positioning itself is a problem. Is it like a bike or roller skates? What is it substituting? On road, what traffic rules can be followed? With the vague positioning and very high price, the product did not reach its potential in sales.

'Many forecasts for completely new products are made using past data and extrapolating from that point. Such strategies are insufficient.'

Arjun was thinking on the same lines. 'I think we at Moola may be making this error. When we started, as a small team and a bunch of borrowers and lenders, Priya and Mahesh led the partnerships. As the numbers were small, each call and addition on our portfolio became a long relationship.

Now our base is increasing but our ways of working is still from the olden days. The team finds it very difficult to maintain the kind of relationship that was possible with smaller numbers. We need to think of completely newer ways of dealing with our partners and learn to include the ideas the new team keeps coming up with.

Ved, do you think sales numbers are an important indicator?'

Ved said, 'Arjun, that was my next signal.'

3. **Look at your Sales**

'One of the early signs of movement are the sales. The shifting trends of the early adopters are an important trend to follow. Look at the periphery of your customer base. What are the outliers looking at? What new trends are they navigating towards?

'When every other product was looking at an online option, Toys R Us signed an exclusive ten-year deal with Amazon [6]. They were not interested in creating their own online shop. The early adopters of gaming and early childhood learning moved to app-based and online options. Toys R Us lost out as they assumed people would always play scrabble only as a board game and that they will travel to a physical store to buy one.'

4. **Look at Your Black Swans**

'The concept of "black swan" comes from Nassim Nicholas Taleb, author of the book *The Blacks Swan: The Impact of the Highly Improbable* [7]. The term "black swan" comes from the mistaken assumption that all swans are white. In this context a 'black swan' is a metaphor for something that cannot exist. Black swans were discovered in Australia in the 18th century, thereby proving false the assumption that all swans are white. In Taleb's context "black swans" are rare events beyond the realm of normal expectation (Wikipedia). Examples of black swans in Taleb's context include 9/11, financial collapse, power grid failure, the Internet, and rapid climate change. Interestingly, Taleb does not consider the COVID-19 pandemic a black swan. In his interactions with The New York Times and Bloomberg Television, Taleb had predicted the spread of the disease way back in January 2020 when the issue was still contained in China. The warning that he referred to appeared in a January 26th paper that he co-authored with Joseph Norman and Yaneer Bar-Yam; it cautioned that, owing to "increased connectivity," the spread will be "nonlinear." A black Swan is not a "a cliché for any bad thing that surprises us."

'Arjun was a perplexed, "How does looking at a Black Swan, when it is unpredictable help us predict an uncertainty?"

'A black Swan is not a trend; it is unpredictable, and therefore, looking at black swans we learn how to act fast when such unpredictable events occur.'

5. **Look for social and cultural trends**

'Management guru Ram Charan emphasizes that an intuitive understanding of consumers can be developed by observing them directly. In his book, *The Attacker's Advantage*, Ram Charan [8] explains this among other notable examples, that of Future Group and its founder Kishore Biyani. According to Biyani, There is always a human observation behind the analysis. In late 2013, Biyani noticed that girls in some local villages were going to temple in jeans, which had always been taboo. He saw that shift as a sign of two things: a greater receptivity to Western clothing and more respect for girls. He thought, "If that change is now accepted, then other things will change as well. Society is shifting, and the family is allowing it." That observation had business implications. It meant that girls, and young people in general, might be more involved in purchase decisions. To prepare for that scenario, Biyani began to reimagine the company to include more young people, more women, and more people who understand diversity. "By 2015, we will have a different organization," Biyani said. The overarching lesson is that subtle differences in consumer behaviour exist virtually everywhere. You need to pay close attention to them. Biyani captures the idea this way: "My job is to take decisions. If I don't understand customers, the organization could wither to nothing."'

IS YOUR CORE COMPETENCY YOUR ACHILLES HEEL?

'Approximately 60 per cent of the world's railway uses the standard gauge of 143 5mm. Why? Because it is the US standard railroad gauge. Why?

'Because that's the way they built them in England, and English expatriates built the US Railroads. Why?

'Because the first rail lines were built by the same people who built the pre-railroad tramways, and that's the gauge they used. (Kolkata tram and all our modern metro lines are also of the same gauge.) Why?

'Because the people who built the tramways used the same jigs and tools that they used for building wagons, which used that wheel spacing. Why?

'Because the wagon wheels would break on some of the old, long distance roads in England, because that's the spacing of the wheel ruts. Why?

'Because Imperial Rome built the first long-distance roads in Europe (and England) for their legions. The roads have been used ever since. Why?

'That was the ideal distance for their war chariots to be comfortably pulled by 2 horses side by side.

'So, the backside of the Roman horses decides the size of the modern railway track.

'It was the same when the first automobiles were manufactured. Pull out any old picture of the earliest cars and you will see a design that looks like horse-less carriages. That was exactly what those automobiles were.

'When the innovation is brilliant or the ecosystem throws a major change, many companies still use data from the past and extrapolate the existing data to stretch their core competency to a viable, survivable future. Such a strategy is very limiting.

'Ever since Gary Hamel and CK Prahalad put forth the idea of "core competencies" [9], in *The Core Competence of the Corporation*, organizations have taken this insight as permission to stay in their area of strength and comfort and only make small changes towards the future.

'The Eastman Kodak Company was an iconic industry leader. For decades, it was synonymous with photography. But it got stuck in its core competence of traditional film products and missed the rise of digital photography and printing. Clayton Christensen wrote about this dynamic in his seminal book *The Innovator's Dilemma* [10]. In it he describes companies trying to hold on to their markets and customers in the face of upstart competition and becoming marginalized and obsolete because they entrench instead of recognizing, embracing, and exploiting new developments.

'As we stand on the brink of a future that can be vastly different from what it was a few months ago, it is important to ask ourselves as leaders, Is our core competency killing our business?

'The impact of the coronavirus can be speculated as a not-so-major event in the last century compared to the world wars but it is without a doubt a watershed moment in the history of healthcare.

'For the first time, healthcare will not be about curing diseases. The one place that shows accelerated trends in disruption is the use of biometrics and biosensors to predict how susceptible a person can be to future ailments. Tomorrow like our footsteps and heartbeat, many other stats can be predicted right on our wristband.

'For the first time healthcare has the opportunity to actually work on the adage "prevention is better than cure."

'Imagine if the pharmaceutical companies instead of helping humanity prevent diseases, only mass-produced drugs that show increase in demand? It will be an insult to the true capacity of the biometric innovation and a nightmare to humanity.

'On the other hand, imagine a leader's vision from the future. In their book *Lead from the Future* [11], authors Mark W. Johnson and Josh Suskewicz introduce a new way of thinking and managing that they call "future-back," which allows any manager to become practical visionaries.

'To achieve and sustain breakthrough, growth leaders need to anticipate and shape markets of the future. One important step in this process is to determine how your existing paradigms and competencies can threaten or stifle the full development of a completely new future. In the words of the poet Walter Benjamin describing the painting called Angelus Novus' [12],

> The Angel of History's face is turned towards the past...
>
> Where we perceive a chain of events, he sees a single catastrophe....
>
> A storm irresistibly propels him into the future, while the debris before him is piled skywards. This storm is what we call progress.

BRAHMA, VISHNU AND SHIVA: THE TRINITY OF CHANGE AND DISRUPTION

'The holy trinity of Brahma, Vishnu and Shiva are the cosmic forces of transformation, creation and balance and are personified by the forms of Brahma as the creator, Vishnu as the preserver of balance and Shiva as the destroyer.

'Who is the creator in business?

'Are the new companies, start-ups or older companies reinventing themselves the creators? By that logic, who is the preserver?

'Maybe the company that is trying to preserve itself and fight the new is the preserver.

'Kishore Biyani, founder of the Future Group, has mentioned the trinity in these simple terms while classifying the three kinds of entrepreneurs in his book, *It Happens in India*.

'In such situations, who is destroyer? The creator of the new or disruptor of an existing system becomes the destroyer.

'The trinity in mythology and in business is a much more complex thought process than simply three kinds of companies. The concept of the trinity is that we need the three as parts of a whole for transformation and living.

'The first in the trinity is Brahma, a God with not too many temples and when compared to the stories of Vishnu and Shiva is rather the shy and silent one. But Brahma is the cerebral, intellectual side of the trinity with Saraswathi as his consort. Thinking about business, it is very difficult to create something totally new and different. Look at the innovations and companies around you. The number of imitation or copycat companies is far larger than the innovative ones.

'Apple is one of those true creator and innovator organization. From the traditional phone to then a slightly better mobile phone that Nokia innovated, Apple suddenly transformed the device in your hand to be a camera, phone, video player, music player and computer and all on a never-before-thought-about touch screen. This one move destroyed the camera and music industry in many ways. This is because the Apple business model is completely different from the other business models and many times would cannibalize them. This is specifically true for all companies on platform leadership.

'Compared to the linear businesses that we generally know of, where a product is manufactured and slowly value is added through packaging, positioning, branding, and celebrity advertisements, newer platform models are diffierent. We know and are comfortable in this Kotlerian model to success in market.

'Now enters the Brahma, the completely new creators, who work on platform leadership. Like Apple or Amazon or Uber. In a platform model, suppliers and consumers work on both sides of the business. These creators then create complementary groups that thrive on the business. Look at the thousands of sellers on Amazon or the Taxi drivers of Uber or even the average Joe letting his room on rent on Airbnb.

'Jaspreet Bhindra in his interesting book, *The Tech Whisperer* [13], writes about the Tweet of Brian Chesky, cofounder of Airbnb: "Marriott wants to add 30,000 rooms this year. We will add that in the next 2 weeks." This super-scalability (think Uber) enables hyper growth, high ROIs and massive disruption.

'So when you know this is how brilliant and radical creation happens, why are there so few companies in this range?

'Here is the leadership question. Most companies will not take this kind of risk to start something never heard of and try to move the entire human population. Who would have thought anyone can write a book and publish? Who would think amateurs can shoot films and they will be sharing the screen space with creations from the gigantic production houses of Warner Brothers and Pixar and MGM? Netflix did.'

THE FRAGILITY OF BRAHMA AND THE NEED FOR VISHNU

'According to Nietzsche, the opposite of creation and destruction is stagnation [14].

'Thus, for Nietzsche, the main example of the "preserver type" in Zarathustra is the human type he describes as "the good and the just." These characters are fundamentally pathological profiles and personify the idea of preservation, stagnation, paralysis and decline.

'In reality, life and business are a lot more complex and are lived between the elements of creation and destruction. Vishnu as a preserver maintains the balance in a newly created ecosystem. If you see the Avatars of Vishnu, you can see the ideal King in Rama, the friendly cowherd, a wise strategist and ultimately the profound charioteer of humankind in Krishna. Pushing this to the business ecosystem, preservers are the ones who stabilize the system.

'Capitalism celebrates consumerism. Communism mocks it. Yet a perfect ecosystem is one where everyone's hunger is satisfied, and more importantly satiated.

'Radical innovation like Uber and amazon may have been disruptive for many, but the company and their concept are fragile on their own. The creators can weave their magic but are fragile in their continued success. That in reality provided by the complementor's, imitators and salvagers. In the modern business parlance these are the preservers, the personification of the cosmic force of Vishnu.

'Innovative creation comes first and the innovative idea must come from an individual, be promoted or financed, and finally developed and implemented, not necessarily by the same people.

'Creative salvage is reimplementation of redundant resources. These resources often move to the next best use, as resource prices drop with falling demand. This creative salvage is an act of preserving. As innovators create new ecosystems, an underbelly automatically shifts to preserving some bits of the old.

'Imagine a consumer-friendly India that is directly opposite to the Nehru and Gandhian vision of self-reliance. A west-induced consumerism of tissue papers, use and throw products when as a country we look for permanance. Enter the creators—mobile phones who bring the mindset to buy new handset just because a newer model is in the market. The preservers of the old ethic of durability is embodied in India's tens of thousands of second-hand dealers and craftsmen.

'The existence of a vast market for repairing durable objects, especially mobile phones, remains puzzling for many. How do we explain the persistence of non-conventional, illicit consumer behaviour that defies normative global practices of consumption and disposal? Isn't there supposed to be a risk-calculating behaviour embedded in consumer capitalism which leads consumers to reduce risk by assigning it to certified individuals representing great brands that offer guarantees and warranties?

'But India's population of more than 900 million mobile phone users relies little on product warranties. Rather, informal service providers systematically breach copyright laws to replace and refurbish handsets with unauthorized components and software.

'The other place where the creation is fragile is the ecosystem itself. Most platform leaders do not have the capabilities or resources to create complete systems by making all the complements themselves. They need to collaborate. The combined efforts of platform leaders and complementary innovators increase the potential size of the pie for everyone. Platform leaders actively solicit innovation on complementary products. But the game is complex and sometimes features fierce standards wars.

'To be effective over the long term, platform leaders need to pursue two objectives simultaneously. First, they must seek consensus among key complementors about what technical specifications and standards will make platforms work with other products. Second, they must influence partners' decisions affecting how well everything works together through new product generations. Pursuing consensus and control at the same time, though essential, can be difficult, as other companies naturally fear being dictated to.

'Thus, what is created is sustained by a huge collaborative fabric of preservers of the society—who accept change and also help harness it to the future.'

CREATIVE DESTRUCTION AND THE DANCE OF SHIVA

'Today, the expression "creative destruction" is mostly associated to the economist Joseph Schumpeter and his 1942 book *Capitalism, Socialism and Democracy* [15], where the term "creative destruction" is used to describe the inevitable process of economic change through innovation and resulting changes in labour and markets. As such, creative destruction, as an economic principle, came from Marx, who articulated the same ideas in *The Communist Manifesto, the Grundrisse, and Capital.*

'The notion of creative destruction though is derived from Shiva, the Cosmic Dancer, who embodies the paradox of the principle of creation–destruction, the continuous balancing of birth and annihilation, which is a necessity for the continuity of the Eternal.

'Jaspreet Bhindra likens the dance of Shiva to the cultural shift and change in mindset required of its people. For a legacy company, the single most important and most difficult thing is to change the culture of its people. To do that, many times the existing structures, design and cultures have to be demolished and destroyed, and a new organization and culture needs to be set up from scratch—much like Shiva, who does not destroy for the sake of destruction, but he destroys to recreate.

'But to me Arjun, Shiva stands for the transformation. Here I would tend to agree with Nietzsche in that destruction paves way to new creation. In the verses of Rabindranath Tagore' [16],

From the heart of all matter

Comes the anguished cry—

Wake, wake, great Siva,

Our body grows weary

Of its law-fixed path,

Give us new form.

Sing our destruction,

That we gain new life....

'From our hearts, like Tagore says, we need to accept the disruption and be ready to dissolve into the imaginary cells like the caterpillar in a cocoon and emerge transformed. Otherwise unfortunately we may stagnate. Think about it, Arjun, in 2009 during the Asian Games, Indian tourism came up with the idea of Atithi devo bhava'—a concept to host and allow guest to come and stay in your houses as we do not have enough hotel rooms. The political and cultural doorkeepers did not allow such an idea to flourish. During the same period, cofounders, Brian Chesky, Joe Gebbia, and Nathan Blecharczyk began the biggest transformation in hospitality—Airbnb.

'Our ability to look at trends creatively is responsive to disruption and race towards them will decide our leadership mettle in the future.'

ARJUN'S DIARY: MY LEADERSHIP MASTERSTROKE

Reflect on how I can lead my people and my company when the changes are so unpredictable and fast. Manage the Brahma, Vishnu and Shiva of innovation and disruption in balance. As a leader predict the distance between the noose on my work and my strategy or product. Analyse the anatomy of uncertainty in my industry and anticipate the changes of disruption by looking at the triggers. Identify specific skills and work styles that will fit in my future plan and current team structure, and recruit accordingly.

REFERENCES

1. Covey SR, Whitman B. Predictable results in unpredictable times: How to win in any environment. Salt Lake City, UT: FranklinCovey; 2015.

2. Bhave A. Online courses pave way to MIT. Available from: http://news.mit.edu/2017/online-courses-paved-the-way-to-mit-graduation-amol-bhave-0606

3. Gennep AV. The rites of passage. 2nd ed. Chicago, IL: University of Chicago Press; 2019 May 24.

4. Anthony SD. Kodak's downfall wasn't about technology. Harv Bus Rev. 2016.

5. Hartung A. The reason why Google Glass, Amazon Fire Phone and Segway all failed. *Forbes*. Available from: https://www.forbes.com/sites/adamhartung/2015/02/12/the-reason-why-google-glass-amazon-firephone-and-segway-all-failed/#316af3ec05c4

6. Griswold A. A dot-com era deal with Amazon marked the beginning of the end for Toys R Us. Quartz Magazine. Available from: https://qz.com/1080389/a-dot-com-era-deal-with-amazon-marked-the-beginning-of-the-end-for-toys-r-us/

7. Avishai B. The pandemic isn't a black swan but a portent of a more fragile global system. Available from: https://www.newyorker.com/news/daily-comment/the-pandemic-isnt-a-black-swan-but-a-portent-of-a-more-fragile-global-system

8. Charan R. Excerpt: The attacker's advantage. Available from: https://www.livemint.com/Leisure/N75XPx78E4G3O5vfLsY4cO/Excerpt-The-Attackers-Advantage.html

9. Hamel G, Prahalad CK. The core competence of the corporation. Harv Bus Rev. 1990 Jun.

10. Christensen C. The innovator's dilemma: The revolutionary book that will change the way you do business. Reprint. New York, NY: Harper Business; 2011 Oct 4.

11. Johnson MW, Suskewicz J. Lead from the future. Boston, MA: Harvard Business Review Press; 2020.

12. Benjamin W. Theses on the philosophy of history. In: Harry Zohn, translator. Illuminations. New York, NY: Schocken Books; 1969.

13. Bhindra J. The tech whisperer: On digital transformation and the technologies that enable it. London: Penguin Portfolio; 2019.

14. Nietzsche F. Thus spoke Zarathrustra. London: Penguin Classics; 1974.

15. Schumpeter J. Capitalism, socialism and democracy. London: Routledge Classics; 2010.

16. Tagore R. The awakening of Siva. In: Radice W., translator. Selected poems of Rabindranath Tagore. London: Penguin Classics; 2005.

9 OWN YOUR PEOPLE

The first peace, which is the most important, is that which comes within the souls of people when they realize their relationship, their oneness, with the universe and all its powers, and when they realize that at the centre of the universe dwells Wakan-Tanka, and that this centre is really everywhere, it is within each of us. This is the real peace, and the others are but reflections of this.

The second peace is that which is made between two individuals, and the third is that which is made between two nations.

But above all you should understand that there can never be peace between nations until there is known that true peace, which, as I have often said, is within the souls of men.

—Nicholas Black Elk

Arjun read the insightful words on Ved's office wall. 'According to this saying, we have crossed the first peace and we still have second and third I see.'

Ved nodded, 'we are now moving towards the second peace like Black Elk puts it but the path is not easy.'

'A hero's quest should have a few slain dragons and crossing mythical mountains or else the journey is not heroic enough.' Remarked Arjun.

'Very true. The second peace has two huge dragons in its path, the leader and the follower.'

TAMING THE LEADER DRAGON

'One of the intriguing things about leadership is that the more closely you look at it as a concept, the more it seems to recede.

What exactly is leadership? Is leadership the same in politics as it is in business? Can you be a leader without a leadership title? Can you have a leadership title and not be a leader? How do you come to recognize yourself as a leader and (more importantly) persuade other people to accept you as one?

'The traditional view of management, back in 1977, writes Abraham Zaleznik [1], centred on organizational structure and processes. Managerial development at the time focused exclusively on building competence, control, and the appropriate balance of power. That view, Zaleznik argued, omitted the essential leadership elements of inspiration, vision, and human passion—which drive corporate success.

'The difference between managers and leaders, he wrote, lies in the conceptions they hold, deep in their psyches, of chaos and order. Managers embrace process, seek stability and control, and instinctively try to resolve problems quickly—sometimes before they fully understand a problem's significance. Leaders, in contrast, tolerate chaos and lack of structure and are willing to delay closure in order to understand the issues more fully. In this way, Zaleznik argued, business leaders have much more in common with artists, scientists, and other creative thinkers than they do with managers. Organizations need both managers and leaders to succeed, but developing both requires a reduced focus on logic and strategic exercises in favour of an environment where creativity and imagination are permitted to flourish.

'From that time in 1977 when Zalezik wrote the article to now, while the world is rapidly changing, man is still the same. And although the context of leadership has dramatically changed over the centuries, the content of leadership hasn't.

'Unfortunately, with rising competition, increased pressure to succeed and the proliferating changes organizations have morphed into warring zones. Success is measured in a share of pie basis and the metaphors we use are slowly degenerative. The idea of looking at the world as antagonistic to mankind, and having to battle it out and win it over to exploit is the cause of the predicament we are in: Global warming, pesticide-ridden food, genetically modified life, wars for control of resources and people, financial systems that are fundamentally exploitative and many more.

'The current VUCA model is a military model, one that has been developed in response to terrorism and urban warfare by the US military. How can the ideas that come from a system whose main goal is to identify and destroy the enemy be meaningful at a time when we have to find very different approaches to the use of resources from the ones that have served us so far?

'As Mary Zimmerman in *The Arabian Nights* says: "It is a precondition of war that we view other people as fundamentally different from ourselves. It is a precondition of literature that we view other people as fundamentally the same." [2]

'Leading should not be like you have a machete strapped to your chest, your safari suit on, and are charging into the jungle. Do I want to look at leadership through the lens of a uniformed soldier, high on energy wanting to vanquish the enemy, whoever that may be in the business world or do I want to look at leadership in essence as a nurturer, providing social and emotional support, harnessing individual skills and stories to build a community?

'Military leadership has its benefits, ones that cannot be denied. The disciple, the rigorous and the focus on execution are lessons that can be learnt from the military way of life. But the purpose of an army is completely different.

'The military rules, way of life and leadership is about survival. Survival in the face of enemies, survival when there are explosions around you, survival when the conditions are inhuman. This automatically means that the focus of the leadership will be reduced to what needs to be done in moments of great calamity and how to come out alive.

'The military is based on the principle of authoritarian control while civilian society of which business is an important is more evolutionary and based on cultural conviction of integration. The authoritarian military way leads to the creation of rigid mental divisions, a static vision of the future and a deep dependence on order that is imposed looking out for combat always.

'On the other hand cultural growth has its guiding principles in evolution. Any single ant wandering on its own has no significance but a line of them from the tree to the honey pot makes sense. But there is no sergeant ant telling them how to form and fall into that line. This is the kind of self-creating coherence that the great visionary Mary Parker Follet wanted for democracy.

'Leadership should celebrate this interdependence that can see the chaos around and understand that something is evolving instead of imposing rules to stay in a static line. So in a way let's just say the military is from Mars and the civilians are from Venus. And VUCA or not, uncertain times cannot be overcome with attitudes of combat. The military exists so that civilians nurture.

'This is the first dragon to be slain. To stop looking at the world through sniper lens and to start looking at the same world through Alice's looking glass, in wonder and magic and with a deep sense of oneness.'

TEACHING THE FOLLOWER DRAGON

'The second dragon of course is fierce in its rigid ways—the follower who still has not found his first peace. This is a concept best explained in Plato's *Allegory of the Cave* [3].

'Imagine a group of prisoners who have been chained since they were children in an underground cave. Their hands, feet and necks are chained so that they are unable to move. All they can see in front of them, for their entire lives, is the back wall of the cave. Behind the prisoners is a fire, and between them is a raised walkway. People outside the cave walk along this walkway carrying things on their head including animals, plants, wood and stone. The prisoners only see the shadows of objects that pass behind them and slowly form words and meaning for their images. This is what the prisoners think is real because this is all they have ever experienced; reality for them is an interpretive existence viewing the world as a type of puppet show on the wall of a cave, created by shadows of objects and figures.

'One of the prisoners then escapes from their bindings and leaves the cave. He is shocked at the world he discovers outside the cave and does not believe it can be real. As he becomes used to his new surroundings, he realizes that his former view of reality was wrong. He begins to understand his new world, and sees that the sun is the source of life and goes on an intellectual journey where he discovers beauty and meaning. He sees that his former life and the guessing game they played were useless.

'The prisoner returns to the cave, to inform the other prisoners of his findings. They do not believe him and threaten to kill him if he tries to set them free. The prisoners think that he is dangerous because the information that he tells them is so abstract and opposed to what they know. The prisoners choose not to be free because they are comfortable in their own world of ignorance, and they are hostile to people who want to give them an alternative view of the world.

'The allegory provides us the typical way followers might react when the command in leadership is top-down. The only way for them to accept the new ways would be if they experience it themselves, they travel the journey with the leader. The Chinese sage Chuang Tzu said, in the fourth century BC, "How shall I talk of the sea to the frog that has never left its pond?"'

Arjun was taken in by this allegory. 'I agree. There are times when a few can see the solution but the team does not accept. It is like those 3D optical illusion images; only a few can see the true picture while the others only see random images. Explaining the image will do nothing till the person is able to see the 3D image himself. The question is how do we as leaders make such a vision possible?'

'Before you dive into your role, sit back a bit and imagine the butterfly.

'Ask any ten people about an example of transformation and you will always hear the story of the butterfly. The bright colour-ed, charismatic butterfly that emerges out of the ugly larva and the inert chrysalis. You all want to be the butterfly. Transformed, metamorphosed and a leader.

'Do you want to know how to become that butterfly?

'How long will it take? What should you do?

'And that is the wrong question.

'For generations we have been taught that the butterfly is the charismatic leader. Be like him.

'Wrong.

'The butterfly is actually a metamorphosed larva. The larva forms a soft sacred place—the chrysalis for its metamorphosis. Unlike a simple process of growth for us humans where we grow in size or develop new features on top of our existing ones, the larva does not just pop out wings. It first totally disintegrates to a glob of imaginal cells. From this glob emerges a new organism, the butterfly. That is why we grow but the butterfly metamorphoses.

'How could the butterfly do that?

'Because of the chrysalis. The soft inert place aids transforma-tion, gives freedom and protection for the larva to disintegrate and slowly pick up the pieces to become the butterfly. The trans-formation happens in the cocoon, the chrysalis. It is the sacred, soft chrysalis that allows for the transformation and helps you in your journey.

'The journey of the caterpillar is the leadership, not the butterfly.

'A leader is not a poster boy for dreams. Leadership is a journey. It allows teams to collaborate, debate, make mistakes, experi-ence, learn, unlearn and relearn and become a better version of themselves. Leader is that person who embarked on the journey towards such a transformation.'

Arjun interrupted, 'Oh Ved, but in my place everyone wants to be the butterfly.'

'In times when everyone wants to be a leader, when there are virtual teams, the rising gig economy, shorter delivery cycles, flatter organizations, the idea that everyone can become a leader is also a possibility. Have you wondered what would it mean for everyone to be a leader?'

'Chaos? People telling how to do things from all sides and productivity and engagement will hit the roof.' Replied Arjun promptly.

Ved laughed. 'No, it means you the leader need to become the cocoon, the chrysalis where all the caterpillars can transform into the butterfly. We all know Helen Keller the butterfly, but let us understand Annie Sullivan the chrysalis that developed this butterfly [4].

'As Helen Keller's teacher, Annie Sullivan changed the way Keller lived and learned, from an enraged and caged wild thing to an articulate and learned human being, ultimately giving her the tools to become an influential educator and public intellectual. Sullivan's greatest gift to Keller was her curiosity: What if she did it differently? What if she tricked Helen into learning? So tricked into learning, Keller became a force to be reckoned with, a leader in her own right.

'Such curiosity is the key to long-term solutions to our complex global problems, when we sometimes seem as frustrated and inarticulate as Keller. Keller became curious about the world and its powers, and listened not only to the men and women she encountered, but also to her dreams, in which she could see and hear. Of her dreams, Keller later wrote: "Perhaps they are the ghosts of thoughts that once inhabited the mind of an ancestor. At other times the things I have learned and the things I have been taught, drop away, as the lizard sheds its skin."

'Physicists today acknowledge that "complexity is the nature of things." Since complexity is the playground of change, the leader can be of great service as we seek to find our way. Now is the time to open up our leadership habits and values to include an appreciation of the possibilities in chaos and embrace the leader as an essential member of our internal life and our external leadership teams.'

Arjun paused the discussion to collect his thoughts. 'So Ved, as I understand the first peace is me going through the transformation to become the butterfly and second peace is to move back to become the cocoon where everyone else on my team can also transform.'

'Very much so Arjun, it is a leader's duty to go back to being a cocoon. In a way if you see, the world at large including all our businesses is going through a transformation. We are in this cocoon together and only those allowed to transform will successfully emerge. You heard the transformation of Helen Keller, if you see there are many such caterpillars all around us. The generations are changing rapidly, ways of working has changed and most important change is the business ecosystem itself.'

LEADER–FOLLOWER CONTINUUM AND THE SHIFTS IN FOLLOWERSHIPS

'While the emphasis on leadership and the leader himself is very high in coaching, workshops and books, the same importance is not given to the followers. In recent times there has been great transformations in the followers—a follower shift of three kinds— people, process and ecosystem.'

THE PEOPLE FOLLOWER SHIFT

'Today the understanding about leadership has shifted from a focus on the individual "leader" toward the collective act of "leadership." This includes the kinds of followers and the ecosystem that is built around them.

'Iksha is an emerging generation follower. He is 28 years old, unmarried and wants to tour the world for his 30th birthday. He

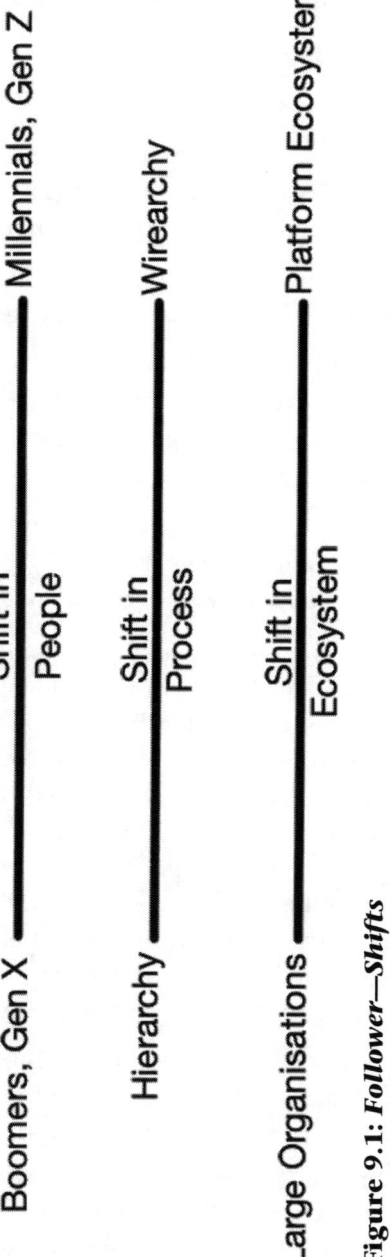

Figure 9.1: Follower—Shifts

has been in his current position for 3 years now and feels he is ready for the next career leap. He has set his aspirations to join the C suite in 10 years and is simultaneously working towards financial independence.

'He is a motivated, energetic team member and believes in collaborative work. He is more adaptable to change and prefers flexibility to structure that is often emphasized by his more tenured peers.

'He believes in fostering connections between people of all levels and all backgrounds in the most efficient routes possible.

'His communication is a lot less formal, he is comfortable with technology and he loves the Internet like a family member. In fact the Internet has been his biggest educator in life. Helicopter parents, video games, social media and online communities have shaped the person he is.

'Yes, Ikshaa is a millennial, gender neutral, and is currently the largest generation group in every organization.

'These are India's millennials, midnight's grandchildren as Mark Hanmant calls them and are the largest millennial population in the world. The sheer number of India's 18- to 35-year-olds doubtlessly will hold significant sway over the country's immediate economic future. By the year 2026, 64.8% of India's population would be in the working age of 15–64 years. A rising start-up culture and the fading craze for professional degrees have opened up newer opportunities and hope for the millennials in India. Indian workplaces are experiencing a period of transition. Office cubicles and meeting rooms are now battlegrounds on which the clash of traditional and modernity is being played out.

'So my question Arjun, before we move on is, in today's shifting landscape, what practices and conditions will optimize the development of a successful working environment?'

Arjun could relate to what Ved explained. His own company has a rising number of employees in the emerging generation and one of the leadership issues was that they could not make them follow the company culture. Now it would seem that understanding the changing follower shifts is probably the first step.

SHIFT TOWARDS CONNECTION

'The current generation has stumbled on an incredibly powerful and important model for changing the world and the workplace: the network. Millennials galvanize people. That's just the way they're oriented to the world. These are people who, every time you ask a question, flip open their mobile, saying, "Whom do I know who knows this? Who do I know who has done this before? Who do I know that I need to connect you with?" They love connecting you with people, because they're all about the people. With the ubiquity of new media platforms and online communities, our connective capabilities allow more than just developing a large social circle.'

SHIFT TOWARDS INCLUSION

'The millennials believe strongly in inclusion and this forms their second important trait.

'The millennial leader will not be the "hero CEO" of the 20th century. Rather than taking a detached, top-down approach, tomorrow's CEOs will foster a balanced power structure, supporting workplaces that value fairness, integrity, openness, teamwork and empathy. As the millennials flood leadership ranks, their perspectives will demand a shift in traditional diversity and inclusion models. For them, walking into an office lobby and seeing all types of people is a given. They are much more concerned with cognitive diversity, or diversity of thoughts, ideas, and philosophies, and in solving business problems through a culture of collaboration. For millennials, inclusion isn't just about getting people of different creeds in a room. It's about connecting these individuals, forming teams on which everyone has a say, and capitalizing on a variety of perspectives in order to make a stronger business impact. This approach is natural for millennials, who are the generational by products of the digital, social, and mobile age.'

SHIFT TOWARDS WHOLE LIFE BALANCE

'And growing in the world of social media, they have better entrepreneurial abilities.

'Raghav began reviewing his toys on YouTube when he was 12. By 16, he was reviewing video games and had 2 lakh subscribers bringing in a huge load of money and learnings every month. What do you think will be Raghav's expectation when he joins the traditional workforce in 6 years' time? Entrepreneurship is not necessarily defined as a full-time pursuit. In the millennial and especially gen Z generations, there are many with so-called 'side hustles', some type of profit-making venture outside of their full-time job. Self-advocacy is rooted in understanding and pursuing one's full potential, passion, and purpose.

'And that is what's driving youth today—potential, passion and purpose over a pay cheque. While we all need to make a living to survive, millennials and especially gen Z are more willing to experiment with how to gain that living. They would rather fail at their own hands than fail to make money because a company took their job away. Same time and effort, different experience. So when millennials ask for challenging work or to be promoted earlier, it's not about entitlement. It's about wanting to make the same kind of contributions that they are already used to making personally in a professional environment. When they ask questions about salary and benefits, that's because they perceive getting a job just as transactional as companies view their employees.

'Also millennials crave work life balance. They also want to be able to work in ways that enable them to be the most produc-tive. Flexibility requires self-knowledge and a level of readiness or maturity to be able to empathize with or understand the needs of others. Millennials view flexibility in when and where one works as a sign that they are respected in the workplace. As leaders, millennials are expected to be open to non-traditional behaviours and to provide opportunities for autonomy and flexibility.'

THE PROCESS FOLLOWER SHIFT

'How can we transform corporate culture to leverage entrepreneurial spirit and flexibility? Millennials view flexibility in when and where one works as a sign that they are respected in the workplace. The trait of being comfortable in seemingly chaotic environment and looking for opportunities in the disruptive landscape is a millennial leader trait. Greater awareness, knowledge and skill help increase one's personal capacity or personal mastery.'

SHIFT TOWARDS LEARNING AGILITY

'Leadership for millennials in the current business landscape exists in the areas of accelerated possibility. The millennials are a generation of information collectors. They have a wider spectrum of information and not necessarily deep. This makes them a more curious lot. Their thinking is—If there isn't enough formal training available to learn what I need, no problem! I can ask my peers, online or off, and crowd source the best answer to meet my immediate need. If there aren't enough points of feedback for me to know if I'm doing well, I can ask my network to rate me. While millennials don't have every skill needed to lead in a VUCA world, asking for feedback is a foundational skill that plants the seeds for moving proficiently and changing in response to the environment.

'Millennials lead best in an environment where communication is a priority and transparency is key. Encourage open communication throughout all layers of management. Then, familiarize the millennial with policies and procedures while also providing them with explanations of these policies.

'Millennials value feedback that is given frequently and honestly. Specifically, 41% of millennials want to be recognized for their work at least monthly, if not more frequently. This makes it easier for them to develop the skills and habits they will need as leaders.

'Their communication is informal and they are just as comfortable with texting as a face-to-face conversation. Their social competency levels are higher than all previous generations.

'In the *Forbes* article "Agility: The Ingredient That Will Define Next Generation Leadership," [5] agility is discussed as 'the ability to proficiently move, change and evolve the organization'. Digital natives, who grew up in a world of global relationships, have become masters at assessing a broad variety of resources and filtering through to the right information—in essence, navigating a VUCA world.

'How do we keep building on the innate ability to be agile? What other skills can we teach the youngest generation? How do we increase feedback and knowledge access for all, especially considering today's national and international workforce?'

SHIFT TOWARDS WIREARCHY

'One thing that's hard to dispute about the millennial generation is that they're a collaborative bunch. The common features that posed as challenges in workplace were the non-collaborative nature, old and rigid process based leadership and hierarchy. Therefore, the millennials instead prefer collaboration, an equal flat structure for sharing ideas, adaptable processes and working culture that is relational. Of course, individual preferences can dictate the level of collaboration they enjoy, but as a whole, millennials take workplace collaboration to a whole new level. They gravitate to whiteboards like moths to a flame. If a new idea is on the table, their first inclination is to flesh it out as a group, right then and there. For them, working together trumps working alone—teamwork makes the dream work. Facilitating collaboration doesn't require supervisors to throw their team members in a single meeting room and ask them to complete all their projects together. Instead, there's a range of flexible options for giving team members resources to join forces and work together when necessary. The most important strategy to keep in mind here is to loosen the control without losing control. Wirearchy [6] is a (emerging) primary organizing principle. As such, it can be used to better understand, instantiate and act towards effectiveness in an interconnected networked world. It works in direct contrast to the much-challenged concept of hierarchy. Coined by Jon Husband, the working definition of Wirearchy is "a dynamic two-way flow of power and authority, based on knowledge, trust, credibility and a focus on results, enabled by interconnected people and technology." Though a new term, yet to find a place in dictionary, wirearchy seems to be the best word to describe all the collaborative need of the millennials in a single word. A similar concept is explained in the ground-breaking book, *The Starfish and the Spider*, as authors Ori Brafman and Rod A. Beckstrom [7] argue that organizations fall into two categories: traditional "spiders," which have a rigid hierarchy and top-down leadership, and revolutionary "starfish," which rely on the power of peer relationships. If you cut off a spider's leg, it's crippled; if you cut off its head, it dies. But if you cut off a starfish's leg it grows a new one, and the old leg can grow into an entirely new starfish.

'In much the same way, today, the followers have shifted to being democratized to become starfishes. A central leader based process can no more work in our organizations.'

THE ECOSYSTEM FOLLOWER SHIFT

'The current business landscape is a great leveller. It is unpredictable, volatile, ambiguous and is filled with novel situations in unforeseen circumstances. The speed with which a leader is able to learn newer ways, adapts, uses technology determines his leadership potential.

'The rise of the "gig" economy is one example of how businesses can now hire anyone at anytime from anywhere to undertake tasks such as web design, translation, transcribing, logo creation and rebranding of whole organizations through apps such as Fivver.

'The very definition of an organization has changed today. Organization, particularly large ones, used to mean thousands of people working together for a particular company. They were employees of the company, they worked only for that one company and in return the company took care of them.

'Today new capabilities are being driven by specific technological changes. Today organizations have become ecosystems of freely collaborating third parties.

'Leadership in these ecosystems, the free-floating collaboration of independent and creative people needs to convey the capability to grow the mutual interests of the group.

'Look at Apple, a pioneer in such a leadership. While in the past a company's supply chain, the people who contribute to their product are always in the background, Apple puts its App developers out front along with its customers.

'Amazon has its employees, but it has a larger network of sellers who in essence work on the Amazon supply chain.

'*Forbes* has around 1,000 content contributors on incentives rather than salaried employees [8].

'Look at the business model of Airbnb, Uber or even your own company. Are your employees only those 150 people who are on the salary rolls? Are you not a leader to every lender and borrower?

'These new ecosystems are a revolution and calls for radically different approach in leadership.

'Seth Godin believes that now is our time to change the patterns in leadership and build collaborative leaders. In *Tribes: We Need You to Lead Us* [9], he argues, "the barriers to leadership have fallen. There are tribes everywhere, many in search of leader."

'Effective leadership isn't generic. To achieve great performance, companies need a leadership profile that reflects their unique context, strategy, business model and culture—the company's unique behavioural signature. To win in the market, every company must emphasize the specific capabilities that make it better than the competition.

'If we look closer at Job's leadership style, we begin to understand the positive dynamics between a leader and a changing enterprise.

'In an article in *Fortune* in March of 2008, in his most extensive public interview, Jobs describes his approach' [10]:

> We've got 25,000 people at Apple. About 10,000 of them are in the stores. And my job is to work with sort of the top 100 people, that's what I do. That doesn't mean they're all vice presidents. Some of them are just key individual contributors. So when a good idea comes, you know, part of my job is to move it around, just see what different people think, get people talking about it, argue with people about it, get ideas moving among that group of 100 people, get different people together to explore different aspects of it quietly, and, you know—just explore things.

'Kevin Hartz, founder of Eventbrite, insists that his company is part of a new wave [11] of businesses that are enabling people to create new economic activity. This is a point reiterated by many young leaders—they are not just innovating a new service, they are inventing part of the new economy.

'The story of YouTube is also similar, Jawed Karim, the founder of YouTube launched YouTube as a dating site, thinking people would post video profiles and meet up on the site [12]. It didn't work until all of a sudden they saw a video of a plane taking off overhead, which someone had posted on the site. A surge of traffic came to the site to check out the video. They changed their direction and decided to make the site open to anybody wanting to post a video. If they were stubborn and kept trying to build a video-dating site, they would have missed the whole market. Being agile and changing directions when you see the opportunity is part of building great companies.

'Warren Bennis is credited with being one of the first scholars to argue for a more democratic and influence-based model of leadership in environments marked by change and complexity. Bennis also advanced the notion of the follower as an important participant.

'Nicholas Vitalari, in his book, *The Elastic Enterprise: The New Manifesto for Business Revolution* [8], says',

> For the leader, the ecosystem represents a new set of assets. Influence is the essential communications tool in a new corporate structure that is, in effect, a pluralistic community of peers, marked by cultural diversity, serving a multiplicity of customer preferences. To be a leader is to influence these others. While command and control, the staples of the industrial enterprise leader, will not go away, they are less effective and can be dysfunctional in the elastic enterprise.

'He calls these new leaders sapient, as according to him, there is requirement for sapient sagacious leadership style to influence, innovate and lead the new Followership.

'So Arjun, you see the second peace is first about understanding who your followers are and what they require. Leading them is the next step. While we see the changed followerships, what does leadership mean in these changing systems? The people, process and the ecosystems have changed.'

Arjun answered, 'I feel like the whole idea of leadership as we are thinking currently should change. The changing followers want more conversations, collaboration, more ideas and innovation. I am wondering what it would be to think like the YouTube founder, Jawad Karim. I remember even Google images started after people wanted to search Jennifer Lopez' Grammy red carpet picture and could not find it. Leadership now requires flexibility, and ability to take risks and trust my collaborative ecosystem of employees and borrowers and lenders and an ability to influence these people to work towards my 360 vision.

'As I think about the changes I need to make, I wonder as an older leader, how do you learn to lead the "millennial way" and harness the power of a generation?'

Ved replied, 'You have already taken the first step, in acknowledging and understanding that they require a different set leadership and that they are an asset, a strength to be harnessed. Now the how is simple, work with them and figure out the way forward. Without your team, any thinking you have now will be an instruction to them, envision your future together.'

ARJUN'S DIARY: MY LEADERSHIP MASTERSTROKE

- How can I create an inclusive culture and ensure productivity is maintained at all levels in my organization?

- I realize my followers have changed their ways of working and priorities. How can we collaborate better so that we build a stronger work culture?

- How do I involve my team in decision-making and problem-solving processes?

- How can I effectively build personal relationships with your team and truly understand them?

- What kind of changes in my feedback and discussion process will better engagement levels?

REFERENCES

1. Zaleznik A. Managers and leaders: Are they different? Brighton, MA: Harvard Business Review; 2004.

2. Zimmerman M. The Arabian nights: A play. Evanston, IL: Northwestern University Press; 2003.

3. Plato's Allegory of the Caves. Available from: https://faculty.washington.edu/smcohen/320/cave.htm

4. Pearson CS. The transforming leader: New approaches to leadership for the twenty-first century. San Francisco, CA: Berrett-Koehler Publishers; 2012.

5. Moore K. 'Agility: The ingredient that will define next generation leadership. *Forbes*. 2012.

6. Wirearchy - http://wirearchy.com/what-is-wirearchy/

7. Brafman O, Beckstrom RA. The starfish and the spider. London: Portfolio; 2008.

8. Vitalari N, Shaughnessy H. The elastic enterprise: The new manifesto for business revolution. Dublin, OH: Telemachus Press, LLC; 2012.

9. Godin S. Tribes: We need you to lead us. London: Piatkus; 2008.

10. Elkland P. The trouble with Steve Jobs. Fortune. 2008 Mar.

11. Kennedy J. The interview: Kevin Hartz, CEO of Eventbrite, on investing in tech (video). Available from: https://www.siliconrepublic.com/start-ups/the-interview-kevin-hartz-ceo-of-eventbrite-on-investing-in-tech-video

12. YouTube is 15 years old. Here's a timeline of how YouTube was founded, its rise to video behemoth and its biggest controversies along way. Business Insider. Available from: https://www.businessinsider.in/tech/news/youtube-is-15-years-old-hereaposs-a-timeline-of-how-youtube-was-founded-its-rise-to-video-behemoth-and-its-biggest-controversies-along-way/slidelist/76111673.cms

10   KINDLE V.I.T.A.L CONVERSATIONS

Arjun sat alone. The ocean waves had become a familiar soothing background melody, the weather pleasant, the hammock inviting. Arjun however was at the table writing in his personal Masterstrokes diary rather furiously. He had a lot of plans and wanted to do so much more with his team. He had already planned to bring his four pillar team members, Aparna, Vignesh, Raj and Mahesh for a few sessions with Ved.

Arjun truly believed he had shed many of his limiting beliefs; he now was aware of his shadow side and looked forward to his business in a new light, not just that of a man who could provide an easier solution that a bank could not.

He, however, knew all this was the first peace. He still had that second peace to go to. Like Ved had passionately explained, he needed to be the orchestra conductor of his team, herd all the people with different ideas and values and ways of working together. He needed to go back to his team and make them see what he could today.

Ved walked into the sight of Arjun writing, his pen flying across the paper. Sometimes long paragraphs and sometimes mind maps and process diagrams, Arjun was unstoppable.

Ved placed a mug of steaming coffee in front of Arjun and waited for him to complete his reflection and writing, swinging on the hammock

At last Arjun closed his book and smiled. 'I feel different now. However I think we have come only till the first peace. Like you explained in Plato's *Allegory of the Caves*, now I have to make my team see the light. Ved, how do I make that transformation?

'After all, the whole thought of racing towards disruption and build-ing a culture of thinking beyond what we know is only possible as a collaborative effort.

'Working on my field of leadership, the alignment of my people and our collective sense making ability is what is going to decide our future. Many of the follower shifts that you have suggested are already visible in my organization. And with the increasing base of borrowers and lenders, influence and leadership needs to extend to them as well.'

Ved smiled in happiness. It was always a moment of joy and pride when his leader figured out the changes and the insights on their own. His role as a catalyst can only be successful when the leader changes on his own.

'Let us explore all your possible issues as you make your second peace,' invited Ved. Arjun, thinking for a few minutes said,

'One issue that keeps propping is the perception that the new and younger guys are not responsible. I know we discussed that the followers have shifted. I am not sure how we can better manage the situation though. The mismatch of the ways of working of different groups in the office is a recurring problem. For example, Raj, my sales head recently had a conversation with his team member Sowmya. Sowmya had approached Raj saying it will not be possible to meet the sales target this quarter. Raj had been a decent motivating boss and had advised her on the importance of those targets and also sat her through a few sales tips. Of course Sowmya was not impressed. In this case Raj did not play the top down overbearing boss. He spoke to her like a friend. And still the action is zero.

'Another pressing issue is boredom. A difficult to believe problem as the team that complains boredom also complains of too much work. The technology and admin guys are the maintenance team. I really don't understand what kind of circus I need to create every day to keep them entertained. Frankly, I cannot change the nature of their jobs. Some jobs are routine.

'There is also this group of very enthusiastic members who come up with new ideas frequently. The finance never seems to approve their innovative ideas in their opinion. But we have budgetary constraints. The recent one of using AI to track potential borrowers was elaborate and completely out of our budget. I approved the plan, as I really believed in the team.'

Ved, interrupted saying, 'Given the bountiful buffet of people issues in front of you, what is the most important thing we should be talking about?'

Arjun responded, 'To create a culture that builds execution muscles and also enriches relationships, one that embraces new ways, is fiercely inclusive and yet when you walk into a room—a meeting, you feel it's your own corporate way.

'I want my second peace to be this culture Ved. How do I go about achieving it?

'How did you bring insight and change in you?' said Ved.

'By speaking with you and reflecting on what we spoke.' Ved waited patiently.

'You mean we duplicate this effort and can bring a cultural change by talking to my people?'

'Let me share a story written by David Bohm, On Dialogue' [1]:

Some time ago there was an anthropologist who lived for a long while with a North American tribe. It was a small group of about 50 people.... Now, from time to time that tribe met like this in a circle. They just talked and talked and talked, apparently to no purpose. They made no decisions. There was no leader. And everybody could participate. There may have been wise men or wise women who were listened to a bit more—the older ones, but everybody could talk. The meeting went on, until it finally seemed to stop for no reason at all and the group dispersed. Yet after that, everybody seemed to know what to do, because they understood each other so well. Then they could get together in smaller groups and do something or decide things.

'So Arjun, if you want to be a great leader then connect with your people, your team, support staff, clients, customers, the public at a much deeper level. And as humans, the only way I know to express myself and understand another human is through conversation.'

Arjun squinted, 'So what are you suggesting I do in the area of human connectivity?'

'Poet James Autry writes' [2],

Listen

In every office

You hear the threads

Of love and joy and fear and guilt

The cries for celebration and reassurance

And somehow you know that

Connecting those threads

Is what you are supposed to do.

And business takes care of itself.

'Connect those threads Arjun. Everyday. The benefits will be visible to you both inside your organization in improved relations and engagement and in the marketplace with satisfied customers and increased market share.

'You need to be a conversational leader. Conversational leader can connect, influence and inspire people around them one conversation at a time. In my experience there are five important steps to become a conversational leader. Leadership is about constant communication. In fact, almost 90% of a leader's time is spent on communication—influencing, motivating, inspiring, harnessing creativity and resolving conflict. The best form of leadership, therefore, is with leaders understanding that one of their functions in shaping and evolving an organization is to consciously address the essential conversations, which form how people think and act. It does not mean indulging in endless talking but rather identifying and engaging with the vital and often courageous exchanges that facilitate meaningful change.

'What does conversational leadership actually mean in the everyday working life of a leader. It first means ANYONE CAN BE A CONVERSATIONAL LEADER.

'Make every conversation V.I.T.A.L.

Visualise new possibilities

'Before we continue, tell me, what is the purpose of a conversation? What should a conversation do?'

Arjun shared, 'A conversation can be the sharing of information or a discussion of ideas; it can be the beginning of a new relationship or the end of one; from telling about a new product to asking embarrassing questions, conversations are our means to an end.'

'Yes. A conversation is a means to an end. A key to many doors and conversation is an essential and fundamental means. If conversation is visualized as a core means for creating organizational performance then the way a leader converses and uses conversation will determine how the organization performs.

'In the Buddhist spirit of dialogue, conversation is not simply a verbal exchange. Rather dialogue comes from the shared wish of two people to respect one another, learn from one another and mutually grow as a result of their interaction.

'The first step is to visualize this conversation and choose your focus. It cannot be emphasized enough that in a conversation there are two people and it is imperative to know the focus of the other person as well. Visualization starts with listening internally and allowing the picture of your conversation t slowly develop in your mind.

'In the case of the earlier conversation that shared with your sales head Raj and his team member Sowmya, Raj had his focus on the sales numbers. But what was unclear is the focus of Sowmya. Without thinking through her focus, Raj has continued to tell what she could do. In the words of Sir John Whitmore, "To tell denies or negates another's intelligence. To ask honours it."

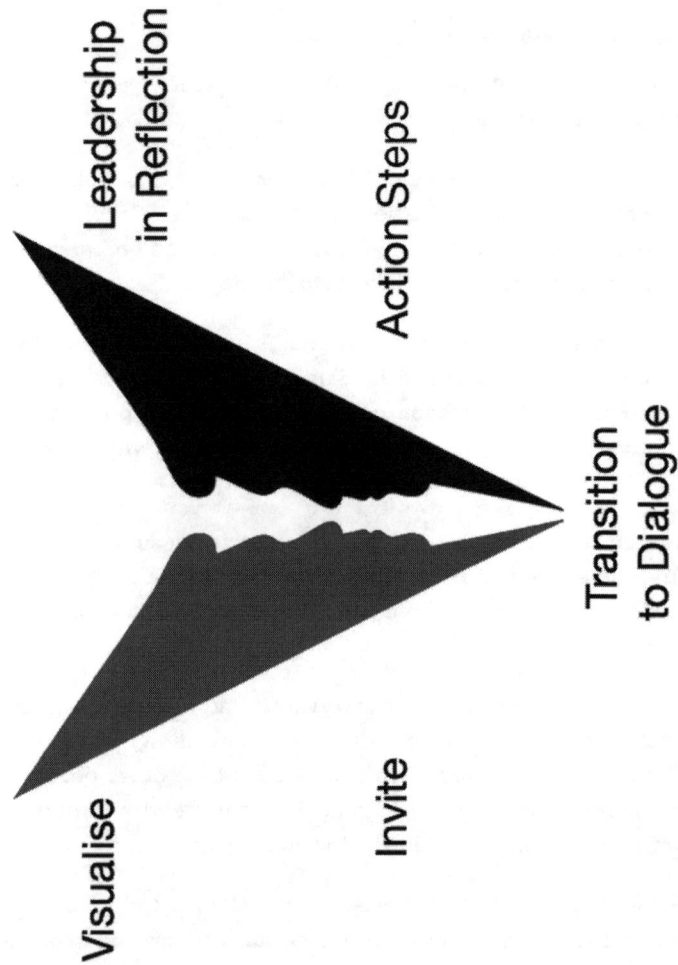

Figure 10.1: *V.I.T.A.L Conversations*

'Now let us visualize the focus of Sowmya. Why would Sowmya, a sales manager recruited after careful screening of her capabilities, come to her boss with a negative approach? What is her focus here?

'It can be that the sales itself is difficult this quarter.

'It can be that her team is being difficult.

'It can be that she is overwhelmed or has a personal issue.

'It can be a totally new perspective.

'By not being able to visualize the space of focus of our conversation partner, or ourselves, we lose opportunities to solve and connect.

'Without knowing the problem, a solution cannot be arrived at and the conversation that Raj had was just shooting empty bullets in the dark.

"What we pay attention to and how we pay attention determines the content and quality of life," says Hungarian psychologist Mihaly Csikszentmihaly [3].

'We may believe we can think for people yet when it comes to ways of thinking and feeling, people are dramatically different. Therefore, visualize the focus on the conversation:

1. Think about where your focus is. What do you want out of the conversation? This ensures you meet your reasons and their shadows.

2. Think about the probable areas of focus for your conversation partner.

3. Ask about the focus of the partner so that the conversation moves in the right direction.

'For the conversation Sowmya had "I am sorry, I don't think we can meet the sales target this time," a few possible approaches Raj could have taken is,

"How best can I help you?"

"Do you want to think through what's bothering you with me?"

"I may have a few suggestions; do you want to brainstorm together?"

'If you notice, the questions are all solutions-focused. It is rather easy to get entailed in the web of problems and details about the problems and talk for a long while, yet no solution will emerge. Such conversations are also a drain on our emotions and leave us exhausted.

'Focusing on solutions however opens new possibilities. If we want people to think new ideas, to reach their true potential, then we need to think in solution-focused direction only. The only answers you will get to problem focused talk like 'Why can you not complete the target?' Will be a problem focused one.

'This visualization is a discipline. It is very difficult to change our thinking yet when it comes to conversations this step followed with military discipline eases the next step in the conversation. Problems disappear to the background as solutions develop.

'The next part of the visualization is to stretch towards what the conversation could become. Way back much before all the leadership theories were developed, Von Goethe writes, "If you treat an individual as he is, he will stay as he is but if you treat him as if he were what he ought to be and could be, he will become what he ought to be and could be"[4].

'By first spending time to think and visualize about the purpose of the conversation makes leaders understand the why of the conversation.

'As Simon Sinek says, "it always needs to start with the why. The why provides the doorways to new possibilities."

'Once you see the power of a conversation as a core process for generating new possibilities, creating new ideas and building new future, the adage of stop talking and get to work will be replaced with start talking and work better.

'Consider this Arjun, if you began to consider conversations as an essential means to co create value in your organization, what specific implications will it have for your work?'

'If we started considering conversations as doorways to new possibilities Ved, so many of the team level conflicts will be solved on their own. The building a new generation culture keeping in mind the follower shifts that we discussed earlier will become a lot easier with meaning conversations.'

INVITATION AND INCENTIVE

'When we are talking about different people, we must not overlook that everyone comes from a different mental space. Even different conversational space. As we visualize our focus, the next step will be to bring all participants to the same emotional and conversational space.

'An inability to do so results in chaos like the story of *Mahakavi Kaalidas*, the Classical Sanskrit writer of the notable works of *Abhijnanasakuntalam, Meghadutam* among others [5].'

Long time ago, in the city of Ujjain lived a king who had a beautiful and learned daughter, Vidyottama. The princess was very proud of her learning. She would often put down the wise men in the king's court. They started to dislike her even though they were afraid to show it outwardly.

One day a group of wise men walking by the forest saw a very unusual sight. A handsome young man was sitting on the tip of one of the upper branches and trying to chop of the branch from its base. The wise men immediately agreed that this man was a great fool. This man was none other than Kalidasa. They decided to use him to take revenge on Vidyottama.

Vidyottama was of marriageable age. She had decided to only marry a man who was wiser than her. The wise men brought the marriage proposal to the king. They also mentioned that Kalidasa was a very learned man who was on a month long *maun-vrat* (the vow of silence). It was considered that *maun-vrat* brought purity of mind and speech and was practised by many sages in those days. The king was impressed by the beauty of the young man and the praises from the wise men of his court. However, Vidyottama was not going to be satisfied before she tested his learning, herself. A debate was arranged where Vidyottama and Kalidasa would only communicate through gestures.

The princess raised her index finger. Kalidasa quickly replied by showing two fingers. He had thought that Vidyottama was meaning to poke him in one eye. He was obviously thinking of outdoing her. Actually she had indicated that God is one without a second. Kalidasa's answer was wisely interpreted as the truth has two parts the supreme God and the individual soul. She was surprised by this wisdom. Venturing further, she showed her five fingers to indicate five senses. Kalidasa thought she was about to slap him so he showed his fist. This time Vidyottama thought it to mean that controlling the five senses can lead to ultimate greatness. Thus impressed, she then agreed to marry Kalidasa.

Shortly after their marriage, one night there was a camel growling outside. When the princess asked her husband 'What is that?' She expected a wise reply. But Kalidasa stammered to say the word camel in Sanskrit *(ushtra)*. The princess understood that Kalidasa was no learned man but a fool. So she drove him out of the palace.

Heartbroken, Kalidasa was about to commit suicide. He was a devotee of Kali. He prayed to Her to grant him wisdom. With the blessings of Goddess Kali, Kalidasa was endowed with knowledge and wit. He became one of the greatest Sanskrit poets of all times *(mahakavi)* and one of the "nine jewels" of the court of King Vikramaditya.

'In conversations therefore, being in the same conversational space is important. Raj may be worried about the numbers and Sowmya may be worried about her team. It is important to set common frames of references before we start a dialogue. Like Juanita Brown in World Cafe writes, 'What if context is like the banks of a river through which collective meaning flows?'[6]

We first need to set this riverbank, else the water would simply flow directionless and get wasted and flood in places. Let us remember, diversity of thought and experience is an important criterion for gaining new insight. In practice it is a very delicate process to keep an engaging discussion among diversely thinking people.

'Have you ever spoken with young kids when you tell them to do something they don't want to do? It could be homework or to tidy up their toys. No amount of cajoling from our side would bring in any enthusiasm. For engaging work, even in small children, they need to buy into our thinking. They need to give us the permission to tell them what to do.

'In a conversation, an invitation and a clear context work as this permission. In the absence of invitation or context, a conversation may have invisible battle lines drawn out. A simple invitation and context makes even difficult conversations a dialogue without too much resistance.

'Of course, it will sound a bit odd if you were to say, "May I invite you to a conversation about the project we are developing. You are supposed to bring in three new ideas in the next 20 minutes." Because even if the words look like an invitation, they are actually an instruction.

'Let me give you some examples of invitation that I use in my conversations:

- I get the feeling that you want to share something on your mind; can we speak about it?

- I would like to understand why my idea couldn't be approved, would it be ok if I asked you some specific questions on the same?

- Can we spend a few minutes brainstorming on how to meet that sales target?

- I would like to give you an honest feedback about the completion of the last project, could we discuss it now?

'Let us bring the invitation concept and the visualization to the conversation with Raj and Sowmya.

'Without invitation the conversation went like this:

Sowmya: I don't think we will be meeting the sales target this time Raj.

Raj: Why not? Listen, follow these three steps....

'Can you see Kalidasa and Vidyottma here? Two people in two different conversational spaces? They have picked up cues of only their worries in the dialogue. Can you think of how the dialogue can continue if they are in different spaces?

Sowmya: Raj I have tried everything. It's not working.

'The conversation that was a very simple one has suddenly turned difficult and defensive. Such behaviour is common in many places and slowly managers and team members constrict their dialogues to only factual reports.

'Instead imagine the same dialogue with the visualization and invitation.

Sowmya: Raj, I would like to speak to you about the sales targets this quarter. I don't think we can meet the numbers.

Raj: I sense you are upset, Sowmya, do you want to share what's worrying you?

Sowmya: I have tried everything but my team does not seem motivated to meet this target.

Raj: I might know a few tips; do you want to brainstorm together?

Sowmya: Sure Raj. Maybe, I should have come sooner. Let me share my side of the team story.

'Arjun, can you see what a powerful concept is a conversational leader? Let us imagine; Sowmya's problem was her team members. In that case who do you think was controlling the conversations?

'The sales executive was controlling the conversation and the team's incompetence moved up from the executive to Sowmya and then to Raj. Now, with this conversation, performance and competence can be pushed down from Raj to Sowmya to the sales executive. Our conversations directly control our performance. An uncreative mind can spot wrong doings but it takes a very creative mind to spot wrong conversations.'

Arjun was impressed. He had never thought about conversations in so much depth. Till now he believed a conversation was one where you were polite, allowed others to talk and put your point through succinctly.

Ved continued, 'It is not always that an invitation is accepted. Sometimes you can ask people to speak but they may not. This can be because they are not ready yet to open up or they don't trust you enough to share their thoughts.

'That is the reason we add the incentive along with the invite. An incentive can be "I have a few tips to share" before the invite "Can we brainstorm together." Many times it works and now the frame of reference for both are clear.

'Practise invitation and incentives to all conversations that have an emotional aspect in them. Observe the changes. In time you will have, build this muscle.'

TRANSITION TO DIALOGUE

'Dialogue represents a significant shift in the way we communicate with one another. Dialogue helps us bridge the increasing diversity found within modern organizations today. David Bohm's ideas have served as a platform for dialogue's current re-emergence in organizations.

'Think about the focus of attention in some of the meetings you have attended lately. Were people trying to learn from one another so that, they could see what was going on from a larger perspective, or were they trying to justify, explain or defend their personal perspective? When the underlying dynamic in a meeting is to learn and expand what is known about something or to generate new perspectives from the views of many, the conversation tends toward the dialogic end of the continuum. And, conversely, when the dynamic is about finding one solution or the best alternative among many, it tends towards the discussion end.

'The main question to ask yourself when you are wondering if the conversation is more dialogic or more discussion-based is whether the main intention of those taking part in it is to push towards closure and choose one perspective; or, if it is to primarily learn from each other and build shared meaning that includes all perspectives.

'For instance, if you were calling a meeting together of your peers from different parts of your organization to talk about a joint problem that has arisen, you might ask yourself the following:

'Am I calling the meeting to figure out what immediate action to take?

'Or, am I calling the meeting to learn from everyone about the nature of the problem?

'When you want the outcome to be a decision, choose a discussion form of conversation, and when you want the outcome to be an understanding, choose a dialogue.

'While I follow many of Bohm's ideas and marry thoughts from Jungian and Indian scriptures, the transition to dialogue, the third important step in a conversation in my view has three components'

TALK AUTHENTICALLY

'The best way to transition to a dialogue is to start safe from as is—sharing your truth, your voice factually is the foundation. This automatically means that you speak from a point of neutrality and suspend judgement, opinions and bias.

'Beginning with factual talk shows the situation as is from your viewpoint and therefore can be opened up for discussion of other viewpoints. This anchors the conversation defining exactly where you are and what's about to happen next.

'In a meeting, this step of telling your facts can be setting the scene, pace and agenda.

'During a feedback, this can be the targets expected and what exactly were achieved.

'In a tricky, difficult conversation, telling your facts ensures that resistance due to judgements and ego doesn't arise.

'It is not necessary that the factual sharing should be used only in the start of a conversation. Every time you are speaking you can take a few seconds to first place your facts and then move the dialogue forward.

'Once the facts are established, it is easier to move to smoothly to the next step—asking the right questions.'

ASK CURIOUSLY

'Learning to ask powerful questions is the central skill of a leader. A right question asked at the right time allows participants to reflect and think about newer perspectives. The question of course is what are these powerful questions and what are the right type of questions.

'Questions that probe into details and micromanage the problem site or advices that masquerade as questions are the wrong kind of questions.

The right kind are ones that open possibilities.

'Socrates was the earliest pioneer to show us how questions that are generally used as a tool in an argument and winning verbal duels can be widened to be used as a method of learning. The Socratic questions are a way to reflect and learn.

'Asking questions from the point of curiosity opens door for newer insights. The way we ask questions changes the direction of our insight.

'The most popular example of a "why" is often assigned to a question Newton asked when the apple fell from the tree. If his question had been why the apple fell from the tree, the answers might have been limited to evolution and biological growth of plant and ripening of fruit. But his question was, "Given that the apple falls from the tree, why don't stars fall from the sky?" That helped him discover the laws of gravity.

'Powerful questions move the debate between different teams in an organization to a dialogue as a single unit. Collective intelligence owes its powers to contributions from all.'

LISTEN DEEPLY

'The dialogue now is in context, all participants are invited, facts are shared and thought-provoking questions are asked. Now is the time to reflect, allow new thoughts to come in and listen. Listen deeply. Listen for potential, possibilities and new learnings. Listen with the will to be influenced.

'To be able to really listen, one should abandon or put aside all prejudices.... When you are in a receptive state of mind, things can be easily understood.... But unfortunately, most of us listen through a screen of resistance. We are screened with prejudices, whether religious or spiritual, psychological or scientific, or with daily worries, desires and fears. And with these fears for a screen, we listen. Therefore, we listen really to our own noise, our own sound, not to what is being said.' These powerful insights are from the book *First and Last Freedom* by the Indian Philosopher, J. Krishnamurthi [7].

'Listening may be the single most powerful creative act we perform; we listen and create reality based on what we hear in each moment. To ensure we are not clouded by our perceptions, our motivations, and the details of the dialogue we need to listen with a sense of detachment. Malcolm Galdwell talks of such a detachment in his book Blink, where he says our immediate responses from afar are significantly more on the mark than ones after painstaking analysis of situations [8].

'Listening from the detached sense makes us hear the whole instead of just the narrow line of words and their use to us. It also helps us listen without the filters of bias and expectations.

'So the next time logic, persuasion, pleading or anger does not work in a conversation, try listening. It will open doors faster.

'Once you listen, you get new insights previously hidden. A new transformation is possible.'

ACTION STEPS

'The dialogue and the learning are a very important step in leadership. Unfortunately, they will come to nothing, if the right action is not taken. Let me share a story that a professor told me long time ago.'

The professor's students batch had an unusual project working for a local district judge. The assignment: Investigate the jury deliberation process and determine how to improve it. As young, idealistic college students, his young team was excited to tackle such a noble mission. The students interviewed dozens of judges, attorneys, former jurors, and other court officials around the district. They asked all the questions you would think a smart group of would-be consultants should ask. How many men were in the jury versus women? What was the mix of ethnic backgrounds? How many older jurors were there versus younger ones? Were there differences in the instructions given the jurors, or what kind of information they were allowed to have in the jury room? Did the trials last days, weeks, or months? They even asked how late the jurors were made to work into the evening and what kind of food they were fed.

'To their surprise, none of those things seemed to matter much. What did matter, it turned out, was the shape of the table in the jury room! In courtrooms where there was a rectangular table, the juror sitting at the head of the table (even if that person wasn't the jury foreman) tended to dominate the conversation. This kept some jurors from sharing their points of view as openly. But in jury rooms that had a round or oval table, the jurors tended to be more egalitarian and their debate of the facts was more thorough and robust. The team concluded it was those juries with round tables that came to the most accurate and just verdicts. The students were excited about this finding for two reasons. First, they felt like they had really nailed the key to improving the jury deliberation process. And second, it was such an easy thing to change. Imagine, instead, if their conclusion had been that the jury needed to be seated with more intelligent, open-minded, better-educated jurists. That's much harder to do.

'They were proud of their success as they presented the results to the chief judge. He was just as excited as they were, and for exactly the same two reasons. The judge immediately issued a decree to all the courthouses in his jurisdiction. Effective immediately, "All jury rooms that have round and oval tables are to have the tables removed. Replace them with rectangular tables." Read those last two sentences again. That was not an error. In direct contradiction to their recommendation, the judge removed all the round and oval tables and put in rectangular tables. Why? Because the judge's objective in improving the jury deliberation process wasn't to make it more robust, fair, or even accurate. It was to make it faster. He wanted to reduce the backlog of cases clogging up his court docket.

'In your everyday world, do you feel you could replace your table? Have you felt the mental buzz of "The new guy isn't pulling his weight." "Sahana isn't responding to my texts." "Does Sarah have to send an email about everything?" "Pravin is focused on the wrong stuff!"

'So it is not a simple balancing act but a three-way juggling circus between getting things done fast, keeping the team engaged and providing vision or working towards a vision. And many days we just feel like throwing it all up.

'Why does that happen do you think, Arjun?'

Arjun had been silent for long. 'I think the dialogue part is a means to the action and a great dialogue by itself is not action'

'Exactly Arjun. Dialogue is not Decision and after a transforming meeting and in depth research also sometimes things don't improve, as the Action steps are not clear.

'Let us look at the dialogue as a divergent thinking process that brings in all ideas into the knowledge pool. The action steps are the picking out the relevant ones and actioning on them. Here the thinking needs to converge on options.

'The simple action steps will be: to first decide who decides the decision-making. There needs to be clarity that who is the decision-maker. Sometimes it is very clear like customer preferences or rising market conditions or government rules. Here, the decision criteria are already set. Sometimes the criteria are vague.

'The actions will be dramatic if the responsibility of the action is shared and collective. As leader, your role is particularly important in this strategy. You will need to make the initial move in shifting the responsibility. Collective responsibility to form a consensus and take action creates both engagement and performance.

'However the decision is made, it is important to chart an action plan. A clear plan of what needs to be done right after the dialogue will ensure the conversation is actionable and engagement leads to increase in productivity.'

LEADERSHIP IN REFLECTION

'Imagine you have had a great dialogue in a meeting. Open conversations, varying ideas and you have chosen a few points by the accepted decision process. As your energized team leaves the room, what are the leadership lessons in reflection that you need to look for?'

LOOK FOR THE TEAM DYNAMICS

'A powerful meeting bring to spotlight team dynamics. And team dynamics can shift quickly. As leader you need to spot these changes and underlying currents. Sometimes you may also notice shifts in power. Dialogues are powerful, they can harness the best and the shadow in us.'

LOOK FOR DEFENSIVENESS

'As open communication is advocated, look for defensive conversations and vulnerabilities in people. It is also possible to see the shadow side of your team as a whole. In the beginning stages, trust may be the biggest barrier and therefore defensiveness can be more.'

LOOK FOR TRUST AND ENGAGEMENT

'Do you trust building in the dialogic process? Do you see people listening to others, accepting new ideas and working on the dialogue itself? Are you seeing people building connections, praising others understanding others?

'As a leader you need to reflect on the behaviour of your team.

'Ultimately, if your team is able to talk like the tribe David Bohm describes, then all actions will be shared and people will always know what needs to be done.

'Ultimately remember dialogue is about conversation and learning from conversations. It is about learning from history and applying this learning in the heat of the current crisis.

'Portia Nelson writes eloquently and concisely of the relationship between awareness and learning in the following poem [9].'

Autobiography in Five Short Chapters

I.
I walk down the street.
There is a deep hole in the sidewalk.
I fall in.
I am lost. I am helpless
It isn't my fault. It takes forever to find a way out.

II.
I walk down the same street.
There is a deep hole in the sidewalk.
I pretend I don't see it.
I fall in again. I can't believe I am in the same place.
But it isn't my fault. It still takes a long time to get out.

III.
I walk down the same street.
There is a deep hole in the sidewalk.
I see it is there. I still fall in.
It is a habit. My eyes are open.
I know where I am. It is my fault.
I get out immediately.

IV.
I walk down the same street
There is a deep hole in the sidewalk.
I walk around it.

V.
I walk down another street.
—Portia Nelson

'Leadership is about making that connection and walking down another street.'

ARJUN'S DIARY: MY LEADERSHIP MASTERSTROKE

As a conversational leader how can I connect, influence and inspire people around me?

I strive to understand what motivates each of my employees through observation and dialogues. I need to follow the VITAL (V.I.T.A.L) model.

I have to encourage the free flow of business, technical and informal information across the organization. Right now this is not happening at many levels.

I have to create networks of relationships within the organization.

Clearly ensure the VITAL conversation model is followed at all levels.

REFERENCES

1. Bohm D. On dialogue. London: Routledge Classics; 2004.

2. Autry J. Love and profit: The art of caring leadership. New York, NY: HarperCollins; 1992.

3. Csikszentmihaly M. Flow: The psychology of optimal experience. New York, NY: Harper Perennial Modern Classics; 2008.

4. Goethe JW. Quotes taken from www.goodreads.com https://www.goodreads.com/quotes/33242-if-you-treat-an-individual-as-he-is-he-will

5. Kālidāsa was a Classical Sanskrit writer, widely regarded as the greatest poet and dramatist in the Sanskrit language of India [online]. Available from: https://en.wikipedia.org/wiki/K%C4%81lid%C4%81sa

6. Brown J. World café shaping our futures through conversations that matter. San Francisco, CA: Berrett-Koehler Publishers; 2005.

7. Krishnamurthi J. First and last freedom. London: Ebury Digital; 2013 Aug 1.

8. Galdwell M. Blink. North Sydney: Penguin; 2008.

9. Nelson P. Autobiography in five short chapters. There's a hole in my sidewalk: The romance of self-discovery. Hillsboro, OR: Atria Books/Beyond Words; 2012.

11 EMPOWER YOUR ENTREPRENEURS

Arjun asked, 'After owning my people and having these meaningful conversations, how can I give more meaning to the intelligence inside my organization?' I know that there are a lot of enthusiastic members waiting to become butterflies. I would like to empower them all.'

Ved started, 'I'll share my personal journey, Arjun. When I began my career as a coach, I had academic qualifications but not much of experience. So, when the head of the Learning and Development (L&D) wing of a large multinational approached me, I was a bit sceptical.'

He said, 'Ved, I am sure you will do well and if there are pitfalls, I am confident that you are brilliant enough to navigate them and still deliver results. I cannot emphasize enough on what those words did to me that day, still continue to. His confidence in me made me feel like the best person in the room and I delivered that day and every day from then on with that feeling.

'Some leaders have the uncanny ability to make us smarter and better. Of course, the jury is out for a few who bring out the worst in us as well.

'Peter Drucker spoke of what is at stake when he wrote' [1],

> The most important, and indeed the truly unique, contribution of management in the 20th century was the 50-fold increase in the productivity of the manual worker in manufacturing. The most important contribution management needs to make in the 21st century is similarly to increase the productivity of knowledge work and the knowledge worker. The most valuable assets of the 20th-century company were

its production equipment. The most valuable asset of a 21st-century institution, whether business or non-business, will be its knowledge workers and their productivity.

'To continue Drucker's dream, we need to ask ourselves, How can leaders make everyone around them better?

'How can leaders empower and multiply the collective intelligence of their team?

'How do we celebrate the importance of every member of the team, every employee having a part to add to the greater whole, empower his thinking and ideas, unleash his creativity and recognize that if we do not do this we cannot begin to transform ourselves as a leader or our organizations for the future?'

Arjun paused the discussion with a question, 'Ved; we have been working on empowerment in my company for months now. From the top management, we keep trying to tell them they are free to take the decision, they can control their field of work and come to us for support and help. In spite of this, the concept of empowerment is elusive; in fact, this E has become an F word now.'

Ved laughed, 'Arjun talk is cheap. Firstly, empowerment needs boundaries, rules and nudge like everything else in leadership. Earlier, while discussing Leadership as a journey, we compared the process to driving on a highway. While handing over the baton though empowerment is not strictly handing over, let us go back to driving.'

'Imagine teaching your 18-year-old son, niece, sister or friend to drive. Would you give away your car keys and say that you are confident in them and allow them to drive? You know your young driver has been a great kid at school, is level-headed and a fast learner. Also, he/she has been sitting in that navigator seat for the last decade and must have observed how the gears work. So, on day 1 would let them just drive around so that they will get the hang of it. Can you imagine the result?'

Arjun laughed, 'Of course, that's an accident waiting to happen.'

'Precisely. However competent an 18-year-old is in studies or sports, he cannot just pick up the car keys right after cutting his birthday cake. In exactly the same way, empowerment in an organization also cannot be implemented by sudden announcements of freedom and open-door policy. While the freedom is for the team, they still need to hear "What's in it for me" or WIIFM. Unfortunately, even empowerment needs to be sold to and motivated to get the best results.

'Now there are bosses that are overprotective dads teaching their 18-year-olds to drive their prized possession. We know how that goes.

"Look at the front and drive. Don't speak. You forgot the indicator."

"Did you notice that car on your left? I don't see you looking at the rear-view mirror at all."

"Brake. Drive slowly, maintain speed."

'Now, we have a boy waiting to speed up the minute he gets the license. Empowerment is not the first breath of fresh air you take but sometimes it looks that way.

'The reason is leaders understand empowerment to be either at the 50,000 feet level and let go of the leash completely or look at it under a microscope and micromanage everything.

'Arjun, you mentioned trying to build empowerment as a culture.

'Telling people, they are free to take decisions and having an open-door policy is only the first step to build empowerment. It is what happens after these policies are communicated that matters.

'C-level executives in a large organization decided to take steps to encourage new idea generation and innovation. They decide to deliberately give opportunities and grow the skill set of their employees. The decision has all the markings of a successful transformation to a culture based on empowerment.

'Unfortunately this is a story of how their efforts failed. Much later the executives were surprised to note that the concept of empowerment was not really understood at all levels in the organization. Managers would give responsibility but not the authority to take decisions.

'The team went on to say that in a few cases, while the leaders did stand up and support small groups and decision that involved driving faster resolution of complex organizational issues, when the implementation part crept in, they found that all decisions had to be approved and reported. There were cases where an employee worked on a particular deal thinking he would be involved end to end in the process but he soon realized he could not work on the important parts as senior managers felt the deal was very important and risky to be given to the employee. Murielle Tiambo who works for the PwC shares her many such insights in her research [2] on employee empowerment.

'What does the microscope level of empowerment mean? It means leaders get in the way of good management practices. What gets in the way?'

1. **Micromanaging:** 'Micromanagement is exactly what it sounds like—someone trying to personally control and monitor everything in a team, situation, or place. There are examples of such managers in every organization who breathe down their team's neck, keep a rigid control on the process, require every small detail before they answer any query and would review all reports, even emails and upward reporting. Often from fear or ego, they compartmentalize and partially delegate though they encourage escalation back up the chain. Jane Silbery might sound harsh but her words can be true, "We live in a world where the laws are getting so tight that management has changed to micro-management to quantum-management to paralysis."'

2. **Poor delegation:** 'Most managers know the importance of delegation; they just do it poorly. Many try and dabble with delegation but quickly revert to their controlling way of working. Such behaviour reflects a lack of clarity around direction, priorities and strategic intent and a lack of clear

accountability. Avinash is a brilliant tech geek and a genius. He joined his organization at the age of 24, right out of college. He was one those few lucky ones to love his job with a passion. Living in a single-room apartment away from his parents, Avinash spent long hours in the office. His passion was well recognized by the top management and he quickly moved directly under the CEO in an accelerated growth program. In three years' time, he was in charge of the entire unit. His hours grew longer, his team was happy but the CEO was not pleased. Avinash was a poor delegator of responsibility. While he worked long hours, his team had become used to waiting for Avinash to solve their problems. In the last year, while Avinash grew, his team has remained as they are. Yes, their pressure has reduced as Avinash takes the majority of the load and works the more complex issues. The CEO was in talks with another company for a joint venture and has been grooming Avinash to take charge but his poor delegation will make him a bad leader. In the months that Avinash was with me, we worked on him building a culture of empowerment and how he can build competency in his team and delegate efficiently. '

3. **Fear of losing control:** 'The recipe for empowerment disaster can be written as colluding bosses who fear loss of control and employees who fear failure. Consider Sofy, a supervisor of the middle school classes. She is in charge of the administration and discipline of 37 classrooms. Sofy is extremely afraid of what will happen to the kids, the school's reputation and her relations with parents if she even delegates a part of her responsibilities. She is also not comfortable with the sudden changes in technology and the Bring Your Own Device (BYOD) ideas in the classroom. She insists teachers make a report of lessons the old way and later duplicate them into the learning management system. The complex learning management system was the most forward-thinking decision by their group of schools and enabled easy access to resources for teachers and made reporting, documenting

student performance and lessons more democratized. Now they did not have to go through her email, they were directly uploaded. Sofy was always anxious and the minute anyone erred, as is often the case with the human species, Sofy found the excuse to revert to the old reporting method. It would take some training and a shift in mindset for people like Sofy to be comfortable with empowerment.'

4. **Fear of failure:** 'In some cases, companies are successful and grow accustomed to success and now they only work on avoiding failure. This leads to a narrow mentality of playing not to lose instead of playing to win. Managers analyse, escalate and double-check everything. Instead of coaching and empowering their staff, they favour not risking anything for fear of failure.'

'*In the Heart of the Sea* documents the true story of the Essex whaling ship, which on 20 November 1820 was on a routine expedition when it was suddenly struck by an 80-ton sperm whale in the middle of the South Pacific. The story of the crew later became the inspiration for Herman Melville's famous book *Moby Dick* [3].

'The ship was destroyed and the crew had only a few small boats. Their captain was a 29-year-old young man named George Pollard, Jr. Apparently, the crew had three options; they could go to Hawaii but that meant braving massive storms along the way and their tiny boats may not survive the storm; they could catch the current and drift to South America but that would be a 1500 mile drift, too long for their supplies to last. They may die of hunger and thirst. Their third option was the nearest Marquesas Island, which was believed to be populated with cannibals.

'As author Karen Thompson Walker shares in TED Talks, given at TEDGlobal 2012, the crew took option two because of the vivid, terrifying images that the other two brought to life in their minds. After two months at sea, the men ran out of food. Less than half of the crewmembers survived.

'"Fear is a kind of unintentional storytelling that we're all born knowing how to do," says Walker. And as long as managers work from the premise of fear, it would be difficult to create a culture where spontaneity sparks, creativity thrives and empowerment is a way of life. In the story above, the three options show that travelling 1500 miles in a small boat is a recipe for slow death. The other options of the storms and cannibals were high risk but the probability of success may have existed. The choice of the crew is not as important as the reason for the choice—fear. The cannibals were probably only a rumour, but the crew did not consider it.

'The military leadership shows high-performing teams that, when empowered, tend to perform extremely well in decentralized models. However in military, this empowerment does not replace the famed chain of command, but works within it, because good commanders know how to empower.

'To getting the best out of people, leaders must come to understand employees' expectations and the ways they want to be empowered. Leaders must be able to orchestrate their peers. They must have the capacity to spur and encourage collaboration and to allow others to lead when appropriate, much as a conductor does when working with an orchestra. Orchestration is critical when working with business ecosystems. The leader must inspire, attract and assure all participants in the business ecosystem that they will benefit from membership. Orchestration also involves creating the rules and systems that provide the common boundaries in which many different employees and partners can create, contribute, collaborate and be successful.

'A leader is not the ringmaster in a circus but a conductor in an orchestra. Both the ringmaster and the conductor have a lot of commonalities. Their work is to create a harmonic show and they have only the flick and swish of their sticks to do so. But bending a pride of lions to do circus tricks and conducting a Philharmonic orchestra require very different approaches. As a leader we need to choose between the ringmaster and the conductor.

Figure 11.1: *The Empowerment Process*

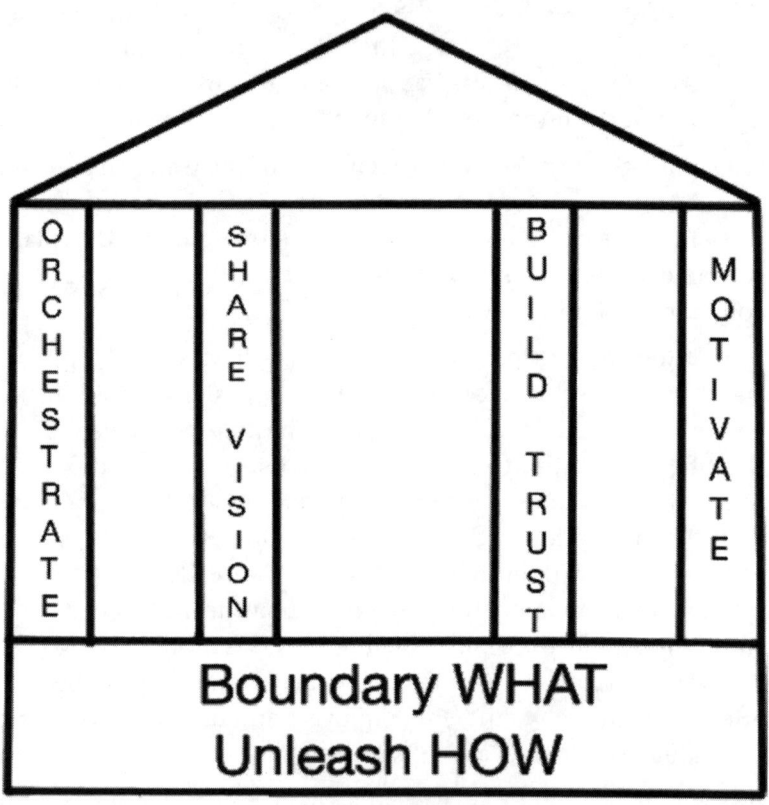

'The role of the ringmaster though filled with risks and requires coordination and incentives is primarily a controlling function. The ringmaster controls the show, both man and animals. He has to juggle the acts and ensure the entire work is coordinated but the underlying individual motivation in those animals is the incentive. Quintessentially, the circus ringmaster is a charismatic top down leader, a great one but top down. Even though the concept of circus has become dated, Cirque du Soleil has managed to revive the concept and have brought to the world a new circus model. One that is far more exciting and exhilarating. In the Cirque du Soleil, even the ringmaster's role is changing to a conductor of an event. It is therefore imperative that we as leaders need to look towards the conductor of an orchestra for leadership in current times.

'Israel philharmonic conductor Itay Talgam [4] in his Ted talk speaks of the role of a conductor as a leader. Comparing different conductors to different leadership styles, he brings to light the brilliance in leadership. According to Talgam, the role of a conductor and thereby a leader is an interdependent journey with the entire group of talented musicians. The conductor himself has his back to the audience and is equipped with only the dull wooden baton. From the traditional leadership lens, not a great place to be. As Talgam explains, while the conductor is "the storyteller to which the whole community listens to," it is the musicians who ultimately constitute the story.

'Great conductors share their spotlight. During the concert, the conductor turns towards his orchestra and when the concert is over the conductor turns towards the audience and takes a bow along with his orchestra. In the same way a leader while working he needs to concentrate on his people and not the audience and when the work is completed, they bring the contribution of the entire team to the spotlight.'

LEADERS NEED TO GIVE CREDIT WHERE IT IS DUE

'Are you a leader that gives credit back to the team? Giving credit to the team is very empowering and a lesson best explained by our former President, APJ Abdul Kalam. Dr Abdul Kalam during a public event in 2013, had said that he learned a very important lesson in life that when the organization faces failure, the leader takes the blame but when it tastes success, he let the team take its credit.

'Former ISRO Chairman Satish Dhawan took responsibility when an SLV-3 mission satellite headed by then new and younger Kalam fell into the Bay of Bengal in 1979. However, when the mission succeeded the next year, Dhawan sent Kalam to conduct the press conference and claim the credit.

'As leaders, we need to understand how to conduct your orchestra so that they work in tune always towards the higher music. Orchestrating the team as a leader requires skills, mindset and a deep belief in your team. You need to empower your team to play their piece beautifully and still be part of the orchestra.'

SHARED VISION

'According to Daniel Gilbert, professor of psychology, Harvard University, "The human being is the only animal that thinks about the future". We have seen how having a 360 vision is important for a leader. It is even more important for your team to envision this together with you. Every musician in the orchestra knows the music. As soloists each of them would have put in years of practice honing their individual skills. They all know what that perfect harmonic music sounds like. They all drive towards the same vision.'

A leader who assumes that his sole responsibility is being a visionary can never inspire others to tread on the path of leadership. It is also important to understand that while vision is a leader's quality, it is not mandatory to hold positional authority for visioning. Unfortunately, the changing followers do not like to follow the leader's vision mindset. Indeed, like each placement in an orchestra translates into a radically different perception of the orchestra, same is the case with perception inside a company: each employee has his/her reality or vision of the company, and this could undermine the common goal and vision of the establishment.

'"Millions of employees walk through our organizations every day not just to get paid but to be inspired by the vision we have for them," says Vineet Nayar, former CEO of HCL Technologies [5]. Therefore as a leader, it is important to figure out what inspires those people and then show them the brilliance of your vision take them through their roles in making this larger vision a reality. That is the way to get shared vision possible.

'French writer, Antoine de Saint-Exupery wrote, "If you want to build a ship, don't herd people together to collect wood and don't assign them tasks and work, but rather teach them to long for the endless immensity of the sea." Vision becomes reality, when everyone is able to see where their contributions matter.

'In fact, Walt Disney once said, "You can dream, create, design, and build the most wonderful place in the world...but it requires people to make the dream a reality." A best practice that can be learned at Disney [6] is to provide highly intentional training for all incoming cast members. According to the article in *Harvard Business Review* on how Disney empowers its crew, one of the biggest learning for the team happens on the first day at work. Regardless of their role or level in the organization, the first class on day 1 at Disney is called Traditions.

'Much before the training in technical skills they will need to complete the tasks of their new roles, the training at Disney is about the big picture—their purpose, which is "to create happiness." According to Disney leadership team, sharing their common purpose empowers each and every cast member right from the start to begin providing outstanding service to guests.'

MOTIVATE TEAM TO PERFORM BEYOND TASKS

'Motivation is one word that has been used, misused and abused so much that it has become a common term, one that everyone knows something about, has an opinion on it but no one really knows its nuances.

'A manager shouting, "Come on, you can do it!" is not really motivation. Consider motivation like channelizing energy. The energy itself is not the motivation, channelizing the energy is. So, rallying for someone may give an extra boost of energy but does not channelize it. Motivation affects the choice of alternatives in the behaviour of a person. It improves, stimulates or induces particular action. Motivating for the best effort is an effort to channelize your team's energy to the best they can do. Let us consider two very different conditions.

'Henry Kissinger, US secretary of state under Richard Nixon, was known for bringing the best in his people [7]. One incident of his coaching and motivating his speechwriter Winston Lord is a lesson for many leaders. In the sixties and early seventies, Winston Lord would write the speech for Nixon and Kissinger. In one such incident Lord handed in a speech he had written on an aspect of foreign policy.'

Kissinger received the speech and in reply simply asked Lord, 'Is this your best work?'

Now Lord became doubtful and asked for time to revise and redraft. After about two weeks of meticulous reworking on the speech, Lord now turned in the revised draft. Kissinger this time kept the draft for a week and then sent it back with a note that said, 'Are you sure this is your best work?'

This time Lord realized something was wrong with the speech and rewrote the entire document. Apparently the back and forth happened eight times and on the eighth revision Lord placed the speech draft in front of Kissinger and said 'Mr Kissinger, this is my best work.' Upon hearing this, Kissinger replied, 'Then this time I will read your report.'

'Kissinger managed to bring out the best in Winston Lord without even reading the report. One of the bigger lessons in empowerment can be learnt here—As a leader decide the what, but don't show the how. Rupert Murdoch says',

> In motivating people, you've got to engage their minds and their hearts. It is good business to have an employee feel part of the entire effort…. I motivate people, I hope, by example— and perhaps by excitement, by having provocative ideas to make others feel involved.

'A similar motivation can be seen in the housekeeping employees of a small boutique hotel in India. The housekeeping team had a lot of expectations from them regards to quality and the work itself, cleaning rooms is not soul stirring for most. How can their manager keep them motivated on the average pay scale that the hotel manages to pay?

'Mr Manager had a series of motivational ideas. The first was he considered himself as the channel, the link between his team and their combined goal. Working only as a channel he could automatically ensure his team delivered their best every day. One link was to ensure the efficiency was always maintained and the next was to ensure his staff felt happy doing the same set of activities every day.

'He crowd sourced an experiential knowledge management system based on the ways of working of the team. They would regularly share tips, hacks, and methods to make the process better, easier, faster or fun. So, it was pretty frequent that the staff would have housekeeping race or team based exercises. The next was to bring in a bit more creative energy in their team. He encouraged every new idea be it creative folding of towels or efficient vendor management. The entire team of housekeeping staff felt that the hotel was theirs. They envisioned the success together. Needless to say, attrition was not something they bothered with in their hotel.'

BUILD TRUST TO FOSTER COLLABORATION

'Building trust is a key element in leadership. It is the heart of relationship and yet majority of surveys across the world report to lack of trust in employees. Typically, trust is assumed, taken for granted, misunderstood and severely underestimated. As the French proverb says, "Fish discover water last." The proverb means, fishes take their environment, the water for granted and never notice or question it until the water in their environment, pond or river or lake starts to run down. In the same way, people discover their environment, the rituals, norms, beliefs and trust last.'

Ved paused to ask, 'Why would someone trust you?'

Arjun replied, 'I think trust is built on the ability of the person to deliver and the commitment he shows to the process.'

'I agree, competence and commitment are very important elements for trusting someone but there is another element.'

'Here goes a story':

There was once a very wise old man, a sage who was much sought after for his wisdom. People all over the world would flock to meet him but there was just one problem. Meeting him was not that easy. He lived in a lone mountain top and to reach that place was almost impossible. People could reach an adjacent slab of mountain but the chasm to cross was deep. The old man would throw pieces of wood. Many did not know what to do with the wood. They would leave it there and go away. A few decided to build a bridge but it was a long process, as the old man would share the wood only in intervals. One man managed to wait till the entire bridge was built. As the last leap remained, the old man stopped sharing the wood.

Surprised at this new turn he asked the old man for more bricks. 'I have come so long in the journey, please share a few more bricks and I can complete the bridge,' he said.

The old man replied, "In this journey, you have shown your competence and your commitment by staying on the course but the last step can only be a leap of faith. The trust you have in your ability and in your cause, you should also have in our connection or else it will be in vain."

'To build trust, we need three intertwined elements.

1. **Competence:** First and foremost, as leaders, we need to show competence. Leaders have to know their jobs and communicate clearly to their subordinates that they possessed the knowledge and skills needed to get the job done. Being a know-it-all is not the requirement of competence or its definition. Competence revolves around how you apply the skills you already have to the situation at hand. After all when we are talking trust, and we have to visit a doctor, the trust in the doctor will be if he can correctly diagnose what is wrong. He may not be a specialist but the fact that he guides his patients to the correct specialist builds trust. Incompetence will be a major cause of mistrust. People may question your competence if they don't get to see you in action. The adage of "Don't just walk the floor, work on the floor" is an important line to remember while building trust. Competence is critical for building trust, but by itself is not enough. What you do with your smarts—your commitment is just that much important.

2. **Commitment:** Commitment is the involvement and desire in an activity, person, process or dream for the long term. Commitment is waiting for those pieces of wood patiently; commitment is completing your share of the teamwork so that everyone benefits.

   In leadership, when you make a commitment you need to treat it as a promise and prioritize the commitment.

3. **Connection:** The crux of building trust though is in the connection. On its own, both competence and commitment are individual characters but trust is a relational expression. Connection is not about what you can do but about how you can add value to others or how you believe in your team's ability to add value. Expectation theories ranging from Rosenthal or the Pygmalion effect to Placebo effect and the disadvantages of Golem theory all point to one area. The connection between the participants in a trust-based relationship has a direct impact in their productivity, relation and growth.

'In 2016, a little after Justin Trudeau was sworn in as Canada's 23rd Prime Minister [8], he visited the Perimeter Institute for Theoretical Physics in Waterloo, Ontario, and announced a funding of $50 million. At the press conference held in the premise, a journalist asked Trudeau in jest to explain quantum computing. Well we do live in a world where politicians and science rarely go together. However, to the astonishment of the audience, Prime Minister Trudeau launched into a clear and concise explanation of what a quantum computer is. Of course, his speech went viral and garnered even more admirers.

'Why the praise? Simply because as a leader, Trudeau, proved both his competence in the topic and his commitment by doing the groundwork beforehand. He also managed to connect with his audience and build trust in that moment.

'The building of trust is only a step in the empowerment process. To bring out the leaders in your team, you need to connect them with opportunities.'

BOUNDARY THE WHAT, UNLEASH THE HOW

'Arjun let me ask you, when you want your people empowered, do you think they need more structure or less?'

Arjun replied, 'Empowerment would mean freeing up the structural rigidity in the process isn't it? So we need less structure. They should be free to do what they want.'

Ved explained, 'Think about your employees and the middle level leaders. They want to be empowered. They also love the top management saying such things. They want to feel empowered and do things on their own. They like the freedom part but do not know how the accountability works. It is just that they don't know the details of the process, they don't know the boundaries. With passage of time, the word empowered loses its meaning.

'A structure is required for empowerment, not to create rigidity but to offer a wider leash, define the boundary. Imagine you are playing cricket. Even gully cricket, what is the first thing you do?'

Arjun cited 'We define what the ground is and where we hit a six and four.'

Ved smiled in appreciation. 'Imagine playing without those markers, it will be a toddler's game of bat and ball. In the same way, we need markers in the organization so that people can understand what a four is, what's six and what is out.'

Arjun was interested now in the boundary. 'So what are the markers and boundaries for an organization?'

Ved said, 'We have already discussed one—Shared vision. While setting a boundary, that horizon or the goal we are moving towards, as an organization is the North Star that keeps the team on course.

'The first boundary is defining what the vision and purpose of the organization is. It emotionally and intellectually captivates the members of your organization and crystallizes their needs, desires, values and beliefs. This is the place we know how many runs to win the game. Let us take, for example, Apple computers. The purpose of the company was to build and make available affordable computers for everyone, not just a few. So Jobs developed a method to mass-produce high-quality personal computers. A compelling vision creates the big picture for your company.'

Arjun asked, 'Where does empowerment play a role here in the everyday decision-making of the employee?

'It sure is empowering when each person in every department works with their colleagues, teams and leaders to translate the company vision into roles and goals that has meaning for them personally. Such a translation of vision takes effort, but it is essential for every team and every person to understand how they will contribute to achieving the company's vision. In essence the larger vision has now become small power units of aligned individual work that can be mapped out in detail.

'At the individual level, how can leaders ensure their team is actually empowered?'

'One mechanism is to throw out the 360 feedback and, in its place, bring in a 365 days feedback. What the leaders speak to their team is an important measure for empowerment. Consider Raj your sales head. To bring in the culture of empowerment, his daily talk and feedback should be on the larger goals. If daily talk is reduced to emails or form-filling or other maintenance stuff, Raj loses the opportunity to hold empowering conversations like what customers want, how can the sagging sales line be pulled up, etc.

'Empowerment is ensuring everyone understands what they are working towards and working at a micro, individual level of how each person contributes to the larger goal.

'The next boundaries we need are the structures around process. This is a bit tricky and most empowerment ideals fail under mismanagement of this boundary. To achieve the organization goals and to ensure some alignment in process, rules and structures are important.

'Consider the customer service representative who answered my complaint of failing broadband service in my house. He diligently logged in the complaint, raised a complaint number and called me for problem analysis. He asked me to wait for half a day while his team checked the problem. As promised, he promptly called in a few hours to report that he is not able to see a fault in the line. My problem of a failed Internet line continued. His next sentence was, "we are now closing this complaint sir, you will get a happy code in your message can you please share."

'The very idea of the happy code was a job well done. My query was still unresolved but the customer care person was more worried about the structure. Why? Because the measurement of his performance was linked to the code and not my problem. Here the structure is the limiting factor in empowering the employee.

'Compare that to a story of the bellhop in one the finest boutique hotels in the world, Kimpton [9].

'Kimptons are premium boutique hotels and one of their interesting customer and family-friendly option was that their guests could have a live goldfish in their room on request. This worked well as children would be engaged and want to visit the goldfish again leading to loyalty. Unfortunately, only the premium Kimpton hotels had this facility and the story revolves around a family who have experienced the fun of having a goldfish with them in their room.

'As the family entered another Kimpton hotel, the bellhop noticed the excited whispers of the kids hoping to see their goldfish.

'Josh, the bellhop assisting the family in the elevator, realized that the children were talking about the goldfish program, one that his hotel did not have.

'As expected the children were disappointed and later the family went out for dinner. Josh was a bellhop. His responsibilities did not include working closely with the family. But Josh decided to bring smile on the kids' faces. He immediately reached out to the nearest premium Kimpton to request a goldfish and personally went to fetch it. Needless to say, when the family returned to the hotel, the children jumped in joy seeing their goldfish in their room.

'This kind of decision-making that a bellhop in a hotel chain could make talks of the empowering culture that the organization advocates.

'So we need the boundaries and the rules but they should encourage ownership and empowerment in people. These boundaries are dynamic and constantly evolving as people and teams learn to manage their work around them. The flexibility creates empowerment. To summarize, boundary "the what" but unleash "the how."

1. Boundary the vision, but unleash individual roles to achieve them.

2. Boundary the process but unleash the employee way of working and dynamic problem-solving.

3. Boundary the values that the organization has but unleash how your employees show this value to their team and customers.

'As a leader, the most important thing is to believe in the process and the people to deliver without the leader hovering around.'

ARJUN'S DIARY: MY LEADERSHIP MASTERSTROKE

What are the empowering questions that I need to ask myself? Of my people?

How do I share my vision with my people?

What are the steps I need to take to identify and encourage the competence, commitment and connection of my people?

What structures and processes are stifling my people and stifling growth? How do I solve them?

Where should I boundary, and how do I unleash without chaos to reach empowered growth in my people?

REFERENCES

1. Drucker PF. The new society of organizations. Brighton, MA: Harvard Business Review. 1992 October.

2. Murielle T. Leaders cultivate followers. *Forbes*. Available from: https://www.forbes.com/sites/strategyand/2019/02/19/leaders-can-cultivate-true-employee-empowerment/#65df6e973ab1

3. Talgam I. Lead like the great conductors. TEDGLOBAL; 2009. Available from: https://www.ted.com/talks/itay_talgam_lead_like_the_great_conductors

4. Walker K. The top 10 classic fears in literature. TEDGLOBAL; 2012. Available from: https://blog.ted.com/the-top-10-classic-fears-in-literature/

5. Nayar V. Employee first, customer second. TEDx Aix. Available from: https://www.youtube.com/watch?v=cCdu67s_C5E&vl=fr

6. Jones B. How Disney empowers its employees to deliver exceptional customer service. Harvard Business Review; 2018 February. Available from https://hbr.org/sponsored/2018/02/how-disney-empowers-its-employees-to-deliver-exceptional-customer-service

7. The Daily Coach. Is this your best work? Available from: https://thedailycoach.substack.com/p/is-this-your-best-work

8. Trudeau meets quantum challenge. BBC News. 2016 Apr 16. Available from: https://www.bbc.com/news/av/world-us-canada-36061712/justin-trudeau-meets-quantum-challenge

9. Stories Incorporated. Story of employee empowerment. Available from: https://storiesincorporated.com/story-of-employee-empowerment/

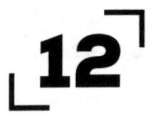

12

SCALE THE MOMENT

Ved was happy. Running on the beach at sunrise always filled him with a quiet joy and today was special. His journey as a mentor and storyteller with Arjun has almost come to a close.

Homer's epic, *The Odyssey* talks of the tale of Odysseus and life after the Trojan war and how his old friend Mentor, guides his son, Telemachus who was disconnected at that time through his role as a son and ruler. We get the word mentor after the teacher of Telemachus, mentor who in mythology represented Athena.

To Ved, it was similar to the *Gurukul* system in India. Be it Parashuram to Bhishma or Drona to Arjuna; be it the divine dialogue between Krishna and Arjuna or the experiential training of Rama and Lakshmana under Vishwamitra in the forests, the concise, practical and story-based lessons stood the test of time and are relevant even today, millennia after their teaching.

Ved mentors his mentees keeping this timeless value that the process is capable of. As his feet pound on the soft sand, Ved hopes like all his other mentees, Arjun would find the Hero in himself and become the leader he was meant to be.

In spite of all the lessons, although they are very important, the proof of leadership lies in its action at the time it is most essential. The real test was in the journey Arjun would take on after he goes back to his company. Ved was filled with hope and it showed an hour later when the friends began their last session.

Arjun was thrilled too. He had also worked on all that Ved had taught over the week. He now knew he had to start with leading himself. As a first to that step he was building self-awareness to understand his whole self, shadows including.

He had figured that he was secure in his state and was in fact afraid of disruption and drastic change. This was one of the causes for his inertia. Arjun planned to work on both. He had mapped his field of leadership and figured out where his strengths lie and where his team were strong.

Like Ved had suggested, Arjun has also been working on his 360 vision. His experience in the multinational bank and his education were his biggest strength that he has carried into the future company. Now he needed to look beyond the horizon.

It was in the racing towards disruption that Arjun is still finding his way around. This is not a sit down with a paper and map a plan kind of change. He needed to go back to his team and formulate strategies to be on top of the game and when the curve of disruption appears his team needs to be ready to ride that. For the next three steps, understanding and owning his followers, being a conversational leader and empowering his entrepreneurs he has been working on where to bring in the changes.

As Arjun looked at all the preparation and strategies he has made for his company in the near future, one thing stands out. The success of all the efforts would depend on how he and his team action it when required.

The last session began with both mentor and mentee in sync with their topic—leadership in the moment.

Ved began, 'Most leaders would tell you that there is a significant part of the leadership that lies in the moment it is discharged. No amount of preparation and planning can achieve this. Consider Naseem, a very positive leader and supportive manager. He had a word of praise for everyone and fostered collaboration and was a true people person. He was shifted to another unit and the team was very unhappy with his move. In Naseem's place came Prem. Prem was the exact opposite of Naseem. He was an introvert and while he did not change the ways of working, he had meetings only when necessary and mostly they were focused on the task at hand. The top management were sceptical of Prem's approach as he had replaced a gregarious Naseem and the team may find adjusting difficult. To their surprise, most of the team loved Prem. They were happy with his approach to set clear targets and achieve them without too much fuss.

'How come two completely different leadership styles be loved by the same set of people? That is the power of good leadership; it touches us, stimulates our minds and makes us come alive. Leadership comes into play at important moments. It is not important which leadership style is used, what is important is does the leader lead during the times it is important.

'Most importantly leadership is tested and tested often. While leadership is a journey, the real test happens on those crucial moments when our goals are at stake and the possibility of outcome is uncertain. Much of leadership is also tested when the outcome depends on mobilizing others to realize success.

'In his book, *The Leadership Moment* [1], author Michael Useem shares the fantastic example of leadership at the summit of K-2. The opportunity to lead was facing mountaineer Peter Hillary, whose father, Sir Edmund Hillary, had made the famous first ascent of Mount Everest in 1953, and who himself had scaled Everest in 1990. Four years later, Peter Hillary and seven fellow climbers were nearing the summit of K-2, the world's second highest mountain. In fact the team were only a few hundred meters from the summit. However, the weather was quickly deteriorating into a ferocious storm and Hillary was convinced they could not climb the treacherous and steep path to the summit in that storm. While Hillary managed to return back, his teammates had refused to return and he could not persuade them otherwise. He survived but the storm claimed the lives of the others. None of the other seven ever returned. Later Hillary had gone on record to say he feels responsible for not being able to convince his team to return back to base that day. In the moment, our actions speak more about our reality of leadership than anything else. This is the true account of our leadership narrative.

'If in this step, our leadership narrative were not good enough, it would be a good time to revisit step 1—Script your leadership narrative again.

'Questions can plague leaders after the moment:

1. Where did we go wrong?

2. What should we have done instead?

3. How can we prepare for the next time?

'But leadership in that moment is something to think about. As part of my coach training we all had to read a similar case study, the famous Parable of the Sadhu [2].'

Bowen McCoy, an investment banker at Morgan Stanley had taken a six-month sabbatical in 1982 to 'collect' his thoughts by trekking through the mountains of Nepal. The incident happens while McCoy was resting during his climb up the difficult mountain pass Thorung La. McCoy sees an unconscious Sadhu. The holy man did not have any of the warm clothing, just a saffron dhoti. The parable of the Sadhu, as the case is named shows us the dilemma of McCoy. He could carry the Sadhu to a lower elevation, but that would end, his chance of crossing the pass and completing his trek; To summarize, McCoy departs after he arranges for the Sadhu to be managed by another group of foreign trekkers. The case bases its moral compass on the various dialogues of the people in McCoy's team and also the other groups of trekkers who stop. McCoy later confessed, 'I had literally walked through a classic moral dilemma without thinking through the consequences.'

'The question of ethics seems to be covered in thick layers of grey areas where concepts of individual strength, stress and support of the group plays a major role in the decision-making. In everyday situations corporates around the world see such cases with their employees, customers, clients and other vendors. Should we give a bit more time to a vendor who met with a personal accident and is unable to pay his dues on time? Or should we move ahead and follow the accepted legalese? From the organization's view point if every trickle like this is given the long rope will it affect the cumulative profit for the company? Are profit and loss only to the balance sheet? These will always be the perpetual questions that organizations need to keep asking and there does not seem to be perfect logical answers to most.

Figure 12.1: *Dynamics of the Leadership Moment*

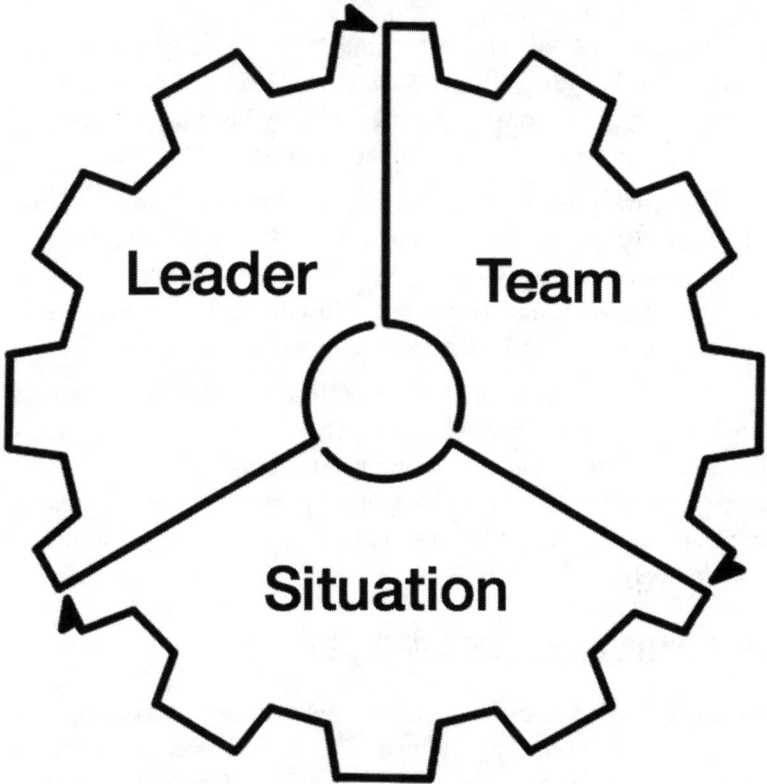

'The one difference in the organizational setting however is that the people are not the disjointed group without rules or set practices and leader. In an organization, there is leadership and decision-making, a culture that the organization strives to be and the principles and vision that every employee follows. Therefore, in an organization there may be a little more black and white than grey in many areas.

'Leadership is exerted in such moments. With the environment uncertain and rapidly changing, today's leaders may not face very different situations from the Everest climbers. Maybe that is the reason a lot of corporate training has now become the hike and mountaineering kind of experience training.

'Business executive Chester Barnard puts it well when he wrote years ago that for executives, the essential skill is "the sensing of the organization as a whole and the total situation relevant to it. It transcends the capacity of merely intellectual methods and the techniques of discriminating the factors of the situation."

'Leadership in the moment is an art that the science of preparation and strategy cannot fathom. Therefore, we cannot have a how to be a great leader in momentous occasion kind of session. However, we can learn how some leaders have shown greatness in moments required and learn the dynamics of leadership through such places.'

THE DYNAMICS OF A LEADERSHIP MOMENT

'One place where leading in the moment has a radical correlation is dance. Dance occurs in a moment in time, and then the moment is gone along with the dance, which remains only in memory. Unlike other art forms like painting which an artist can take a lot of time to capture ideas, work on rough drafts and sketches, erase, rework and store the work for future, dance is momentary. Much like dance, leadership is also not something that you can come back and revisit the next day. If that were possible, Peter Hillary would have gone back to his team and saved them. The act of leadership cannot be stored, prepared and captured for future use. Leadership occurs in the moment and then it is gone. As Walter Sorrell puts it eloquently, "Life only lasts the very moment of our awareness of it, and all that remains is as in the dance, the memory we can retain of it."

'Imagine a ballet. The audience are waiting, the lights are dimmed and then the music begins. The dancer enters with a burst of energy. As the performance continues, the choreography, the movement, the music bring alive the story of the dance. The air is charged with the energy. The audience are connected with the dance in spirit. This in turn gives energy and enthusiasm to the tiring dancer. Long after the performance, everyone in the room carries a piece of the dance in their hearts and memories.

'So what makes the dance magical? Is it the music? The lights? The choreography? Or the audience?

'If you remove any one of those elements, the magic of the performance is lost. The magic lies in the dynamics at the moment of performance.

'It is the same for leadership as well. Leadership lies in the dynamics among the leader, the follower and the issue at hand or the moment where the leadership is required. The importance of the dynamic can only be felt when the three don't align during a crucial moment. Perhaps the wise have always been aware of this.

'Karna, the eldest son of Kunti, yet never recognized due to the circumstances of his birth, manages to learn under sage Parashuram through deceit. He lies about being a brahmin. When the sage Parashuram finds out the truth, he is furious with Karna and accuses him of stealing knowledge by lying and omission.

'He curses Karna that he would forget all his knowledge specifically the ones required to use the *Brahmastra* (weapon) in time of need. Parashuram could have just cursed oblivion, where Karna forgets all that he has learnt but that is not the curse. Karna's knowledge and competence builds his confidence and even arrogance but when the time comes, he fails proving that one's competence at rest can fuel self-worth but leadership is in the dynamic moment in the battlefield.

'Though the nature of leadership is momentary, like dance to create great moments require rigour and practice of long hours. This is the reason that we have the process of building up leadership acumen.'

ALIGNMENT OF THE LEADER

'A leader is the one high performer who goes through the grind. The lessons, the training, the expectations, the goals. He is the dancer who has a brilliant choreographed piece ready for him and he has been practising long hours at it. Therefore, it might look like he is the pivot and away from the needs of an alignment, but it is the leader or the lead dancer who needs to be perfect sync with the stakeholders.

'In leadership, the problems between right and wrong are easily dealt with. We have legal and ethical codes to live by and enough monitors there as well. The problem happens when the leader has to deal with right and right and when one right is tilted a bit off balance. Perhaps the maximum damage to leadership is done by the theory of maximizing shareholder value as a sole target in business.

'Arthur Miller has been among the foremost critics of the adverse effects of a selfish capitalist society. Miller's plays present, in stark terms, the dilemmas faced by leaders in a capitalist system. His most celebrated play "All my sons" has been part of many a leadership discussion and classes across the world.

'All My Sons by Arthur Miller [3] is a play set during the Second World War, and is about a successful businessman, Joe Keller. He lives peacefully with his wife Kate and his son Chris, but had another son Larry who is missing in action from the Second World War, for the last 3 years.'

The concept of the play was to bring to light the principles of Joe Keller who made his money as a war profiteer during the war, with his business partner, Steve Deever. Their business was to ship cylinders for fighter planes. In one incident, a particular inventory of the cylinder heads come out cracked. Joe Keller instructs to just seal the crack and ship the cylinder heads. This decision proves fatal to the 21 fighter pilots and all their planes crash. As the story unfolds, we see that both sons of Joe are disappointed by the decisions of their father. The elder son dies by taking out a faulty plane knowing it was his dad's fault. The younger son Chris, confronts his father, the following lines from the play give the true impact -

CHRIS (in a broken whisper): Then you did it?

KELLER (with the beginning of plea in his voice): He never flew a P-40—

CHRIS (Struck, deadly): But the others.

KELLER (insistently): She's out of her mind. (He takes a step towards Chris, pleadingly).

CHRIS (unyielding): Dad.... you did it?

KELLER: He never flew a P-40, what's the matter with you?

CHRIS (still asking and saying): Then you did it. To the others. [4]

The story of Joe Keller is to help us understand, as a leader who is the true stakeholder? Keller decided his family came first, at the cost of his country.

'Fairness and equity are easily understood in general, but when the crisis moment requires these skills, leaders may not be able to align all their stakeholders.

'To a reader, Joe Keller might look a murderer as he chose family and company over the nation. Consider for a minute, before enlightenment, Buddha was also the confused prince Siddhartha who left his wife and baby son alone and walked out in the middle of the night. What if he had not got the enlightenment? He would remain the prince who did not do his duties. So does his becoming Buddha negate the lack of leadership shown as a husband, father and prince?

'Mahatma Gandhi is yet another example of a great leader who put the nation in front of his family.

'The leadership stories of these heroes and that of Keller show us the need to maintain the alignment of the players and moments alive in leadership.

'There is not formula or theory. Leaders have to build their own frame of reference here to align their balance between right and right be it between stakeholders, between competition and collaboration or between now and the future. Leadership is that tough journey sometimes where the hard choices and decision made cannot be validated or explained at the time the decision was made.'

ALIGNMENT OF THE TEAM: THAI CAVE RESCUE

'The relationship between a leader and his/her followers is essentially not one of reason, for then, it is a merely transactional relationship. Followers need to have trust in a leader, not as the outcome of a process of reasoning, but as a value in itself. Trust is needed to fill the gap where reason has no domain.

'The leadership dynamic and its alignment with the leader, team and a very difficult situation is the perfect setting to test leadership, team alignment and resilience.

'Twelve boys aged 11–16, a very young coach aged 25 and an 18 day long fight to survival and rescue from water-filled caves is one of the finest display of leadership

'The Thai soccer team, stuck in Tham Luang Cave Rescue [5], in June–July 2018 in the Thai forest reserve will go down in the books of history as a moment when humanity displayed great leadership.'

On June 23, the 12 members of the Wild Boars soccer team and their 25-year-old assistant coach strayed too far beyond tourist limits at the Tham Luang Nang Non cave in northern Thailand. June is a season for heavy rains in Thailand and it began to rain suddenly.

The torrential rains continued for a week flooding the six-mile maze of caves, forcing the boys and their coach to move further inside to an elevated, dry place.

'For leadership, there are three aspects to consider here.

1. How did the team stay alive inside that cave for 14 days?

2. How did the rescue team evacuate the entire soccer team of teenagers when it water levels were that high?

3. How did the officials and the government deploy and manage the resources to ensure all 13 members were saved?

   1. The most challenging question is how did the young boys with a leader who was just a few years elder to them manage to stay alive for 14 days? The tourist allowed part of the cave was only half a mile, there were two passages beyond this point and the young coach and his enthusiastic team explored beyond these points. When they were up there, a wall of water came down. The team, of course, managed to stay at an elevated part of the cave. Although the coach, Ekapol Chanthawong, in a moment of rash decision lead the boys too far inside the caves, it was he who was responsible for their survival. The young coach had come up with ideas to stretch their meagre food supply, asked the team to switch off mobiles and use them in emergency to save battery life for flashlight and had also taught them meditation to stay calm and positive. The lesson easily missed here is the nature of oneness from the team. They would have been scared. Of the dark, the rising water levels, the complete lack of idea of how and when rescue will finally help out. Yet the boys persisted.

   2. The commitment and collaboration of the rescue team in spite of the fact that they lost one of their members to the rescue is unthinkable. The role played by the rescue team was also phenomenal. One of the four Thai SEALs who went in and stayed with the trapped soccer team

was a physician. This was great thinking on the part of the rescue team. Of course the operational problem of evacuating the team finally involved pumping out about a half billion gallons of water. Again the farmers who allowed the water to be pumped into their farms knowing fully well that it will kill their crops is another show in alignment to the final goal to rescue 13 people.

3. The role of the officials, the bureaucracy and regulations often are spoken as examples in situations where good work is hampered. This is probably the one place where the government has taken a great step and fast. Narongsak Osatanakorn showed his leadership in taking quick and efficient decision.

'The Thai cave rescue will go down in history as one of these incredible leadership moments when more than 10,000 people tested their leadership mettle. Here the alignment was not just of the coach or the governor, but all the people who participated. This is the kind of alignment that brings in hope and faith.

'We often take leadership to be an action performed by only the leaders. The Thai cave rescue team is a shining example that leadership is a continuum and followers and team members are complimentary and an integral part of this continuum. The success of the rescue is as much because the boys listened and pushed on with meagre supplies as much it was for highly skilled rescue SEALs to work the process. This is the dynamic moment where the followers and the leaders align themselves for success.'

ALIGNMENT TO SITUATIONS: JARED COHEN

'Swami Vivekananda in his speech delivered at the famous hall in Chicago says, "One of the greatest lessons I have learnt in my life is to pay as much attention to the means of work, as to its end...with the means all right, the end must come." The purpose of leadership is the journey itself, not the destination. What will you do with a brilliant technical mind? Get a job that pays the best? Start a company that covers huge market share? Or figure out how your skill can be used to better humanity?

'The place where we use our leadership decides the kind of leader we are. While it is rather important to be a person who aims for the great job and the entrepreneur who creates the next gold rush, humanity also needs leaders who will use their skills for the betterment of humanity.

'Jared Cohen [6] is the kind of man you aspire to be. Well educated, intelligent and with a social consciousness. At 34 years of age, Jared became a trusted advisor to two Secretaries of State, founded a new division of Google, and authored a New York Times Bestseller. He is the example of a student who studies and actually uses his education for its purpose towards humanity. Cohen studied History and Political science in Stanford and decided to experience the education in Africa.

'While most undergrad students would take a trip to the great Masaai Mara as trip to Africa, Cohen made it a true living with the natives experience by living in a dung hut in Kenya, witnessing the Rwandan genocide from Hutu perpetrators. Next he studies International Relations as a Rhodes Scholar at Oxford.

'This time he spent much of his time in Iran researching on how political opposition in Iran viewed the United States. Cohen interacted with a lot of the younger Iranians. As a leader, Cohen's work came to its dynamic testing point during the 2009 Iran protests. Dissidents protested the election results for Ahmadinejad on the basis of fraud, and the Iranian government had shut down cell texting. Not discouraged, the young Iranians took to Twitter to communicate. Cohen knew this information as he had interacted with the Iranian youth. At the same time, Twitter's servers were scheduled to go down for maintenance in the middle of the night. The protestors would lose their only link to each other and the outside world if the maintenance shut-down was implemented. Cohen emailed the Twitter founder and CEO, Jack Dorsey, to explain the situation and Twitter postponed its maintenance. CNN included Cohen's plea to Dorsey in its list of top 10 Internet moments of the decade, sharing the designation with the launch of Facebook and the release of the iPhone.

'Jared Cohen is an example of a leader who used his skill for the people. We have many such stories. Mohammed Yunis who began the *Grameen* Bank is a stellar example of such a leader who aligned his competence to the best way his followers could benefit and at the opportune moment.

'Leadership in the moment, therefore, is to create a rhythm out of the various divergent people, patterns groups and interests and integrate them in time. Rhythm does not mean a steady boring repeated pattern of beats. It can be the highs and lows and gaps in between. One thing that people aspiring to be leaders need to know that many leaders know and yet many do not acknowledge is leaders cannot know everything. Leadership is not a skill or a competence, though they are important. Leadership is a journey. Every station is important; every touch point counts. The means is as important as the end.

'As we come to the end of the learning Arjun, let us revisit the first question I asked. What does leadership mean to you?

'In this long journey of discovery, I am sure you have learnt a lot of nuances but the core question will remain the same.

'What does leadership mean to you? That is your true north.

'In conclusion, let me share a fascinating tale of Vikram and Vetaal. In the kingdom of Avantee Desh, there lived a princess named Sashi. A woman of great beauty and intellect, her parents wanted a suitable groom for their daughter, one who would also become the potential king. Proposals rushed in from many places but four of them stood out.

'Prince from Chol Desh professed to be a great archer, a shabd-vedhi (one who could shoot by just hearing the sound of the target).

'Prince from Vaishalee had a magical weaving ability that he could create the finest fabrics in the world.

'Prince from Bang Desh could recite all the Vedas and Puranas and had the knowledge of a seer.

'The Prince from Chedi Desh was a magical Vaidya. There was no disease that he could not cure.

'Vetaal's question of course was whom should the princess marry?

'In a way all the learning of this journey is like the skills of the princes. Great in their own way but when the question of suitability comes in, we need to put in the dynamic of the situation.

'In the story, Vikram of course answers right by choosing the Prince from Chol Desh, as he is the only one who has the skills of a warrior, a requirement for being future king. The others were good professionals in their field.

'In the same way, Arjun, now it is your turn to practise and rewrite your leadership narrative to the requirements of your organization.

'Keeping these in mind, what does leadership mean to you?'

If you remain silent, you die; if you speak, you lose.

As Ved concluded his session, there was an emotional moment in the room. For some time, Arjun was silent, assimilating all that was told. Not just in this session but all that he has learnt so far. All the lessons Arjun had learnt from his college days, his working in a bank and in his journey as founder and CEO of Moola. Arjun was also assimilating all that is required of him in the future. He could see with clarity the journey that is leadership. While leadership carries the lessons of the past and the experience of the present, it is essentially a journey towards the future.

Arjun imagined a future where everyone led from within, where leaders embrace inclusive teams of emerging generation, newer ways of working and race towards uncertainty with confidence. He was ready to rewrite such a leadership narrative

ARJUN'S DIARY: MY LEADERSHIP MASTERSTROKE

It has been almost a year since my week-long mentoring saga with Ved, the corporate Vetaal.

A lot has changed in Moola. My four next in command, my pillars, were also mentored by Ved. Now we have built systems to ensure everyone first leads themselves.

Self-leadership is a must to all employees at Moola. This is because we have created our system to ensure there is a lot of empowerment and free-flowing conversation among the people.

The teams are now stronger and there is an idea cell that caters to the new ideas of the team. This has been the best part of our restructuring. We are diversifying the business to newer horizons based on them.

The future looks good as the team that holds it is a great one. My leadership masterstroke has been to rethink my approach to leading the future, both people and goals.

REFERENCES

1. Useem M. The leadership moment: Nine true stories of triumph and disaster and their lessons for us all. New York, NY: Times Business, Random House Publishing.

2. Bowen M. The parable of the sadhu. Harv Bus Rev. 1997 May–Jun.

3. Manikutty S. The essence of leadership. London: Bloomsbury Publishing.

4. Miller A. All my sons. New York, NY: Reynal and Hitchcock Inc; 1947.

5. Useem M, Eaves A. The Thai cave rescue: What are the leadership lessons? Knowledge@Wharton show; 2018 Mar. Available from: https://knowledge.wharton.upenn.edu/article/leadership-lessons-thai-soccer-team-rescue/

6. Cain B, Cohen J. A 21st century leader. Vanderbilt Pol Rev. 2015 Nov. Available from: https://vanderbiltpoliticalreview.com/4393/archives/fixit/jared-cohen-a-21st-century-leader/

PART 3

Practising
Leadership

13   YOUR LEADERSHIP MASTERSTROKE

The dogmas of the quiet past are inadequate to the stormy present.... As our case is new, so we must think anew, act anew

—*Abraham Lincoln*

We are on the edge of a new era in leadership. The leadership models of the past provide very little in the form of guidance in the future. Leadership is best defined as a journey. To be a leader in uncertain times, you need to master

1. The field of leadership

2. The journey of becoming a leader in uncertain times with changing followers.

Learning to lead is one of those continuous personal capacities that is only improved with application and practice. As you begin your journey to your leadership, do carry these resources with you. Consider this section as your resource inventory. Dip in anytime to learn a new way of thinking, jump to any section at random or as you need. The resource for each leadership quality/behaviour is divided into three sections:

1. **Impact change:** This is the first section to consider as a leader. Having clarity on why you need a particular leadership resource will ensure your clarity in reaching the leadership quality.

2. **Take charge:** This section is your go-to resource for the action you can take to improve the way you understand, apply and convey the newer leadership qualities. Set pragmatic strategies, involve people and inspire them to act. You may

want to take a particular action but might be stuck in how to continue. The next section shows you the rope on how.

3. **Act decisively:** This section provides you with the resources, suggestions and ideas on how to implement an action. Good and timely decisions are the most important part, as the execution of your strategy is the only indicator of success. It also suggests behaviour and attitude changes augment your efforts and capitalize your strengths. Remember you are a leader everywhere; therefore, these suggestions need not be limited to your workplace.

YOUR LEADERSHIP JOURNEY: THE SEVEN STEPS

A clear idea of your field of leadership will provide clarity on the whole picture. A bird's eye view enables you to see the interlinks and connections better

The field of leadership is your map. It is the abstraction of your leadership reality. Understanding the map will help you to navigate the leadership journey with ease.

Understand the seven steps to your journey. While it is not necessary to follow the steps in sequence, you can jump to any step you want, it is advisable to follow all of them.

STEP 1: SELF-MASTERY

*   **Impact change**
    *   o   Consider self-leadership as the foundational step in your leadership journey
    *   o   Imagine how your leadership will be with great people, process and goals but you the leader is yet undeveloped. Do not be a donut leader.
    *   o   To encourage leadership in others you need to encourage leadership in you.

- **Take charge**
  - o Reflect on what does leadership mean to you. Where do you see yourself as a leader and how do you see yourself leading. What are your leadership qualities?
  - o Observe how you see leadership to be. Is leadership a role? A process? A responsibility? Ability?
  - o Consider who according to you is a good leader? Who is a bad leader? Monitor the qualities of leadership that you consider important. Observe these qualities in you.
  - o Reflect for a while and understand how high or low is your self-esteem right now.
  - o Monitor your behaviours and reaction to others' behaviours. What are some of the behaviours that you have adopted from others?
  - o Build your self-confidence. Self-confidence is the confidence in your judgement, ability and power.
  - o Identify your self-motivators. Figure out what motivates you. Are you motivated by activity? Money? Power? Action? Recognition? Or affiliation?
  - o Examine your ARC mindset. What are your levels of adaptation? How have you tested it? Examine your resilience to bounce back. Explore your curiosity element.
  - o What is your role in the current problem you play? How are you leading towards the solution? Who will listen to you?
  - o Meet your shadow. Who is this person? Reflect on the person revealed. Accept the whole of you.
  - o Test how strong is your ability to choose. The power to be proactive is the mark of a true leader. The difference between Pavlov's dog and a leader is his ability to choose.
  - o Become aware of how you feel and realize you have the ability to choose your emotion and your actions.

o Monitor if your decisions are a result of conscious reasoning or a reaction to stimuli.

- **Act decisively**

    o Understand and clearly list what you want to change, disrupt, create and preserve.

    o Analyse personal dragons and what does slaying them would involve.

    o Define what strengths make up your personal army.

    o Script a clear leadership narrative that shows the kind of leader you represent.

STEP 2: TRIGGER YOUR VISION

- **Impact change**

    o A clear leadership vision will ensure clarity in all aspects of leadership. A clear vision will also help your followers know what they are striving towards.

- **Take charge**

    o Observe if you are committed to transformation. As the business continues to move at unprecedented speed, your vision should be able to shift paradigms and expand to new ones

    o Recognize the interconnectedness of your vision with your people. Today, people want equal ownership of your vision. Evaluate if your vision encapsulates the opportunity to maximize potential, profits and people.

    o Forecast whether your vision holds the space for expansion for changes and growth tomorrow.

    o Explore the nature of your vision. Make your leadership vision circular. In the way post-industrial revolution linear economies are giving way to a circular sustainable economy leadership vision in the present turbulent times needs to be circular – an iterative process to plan – act – listen for reaction – iterate.

o Analyse if your vision is much larger than just you the individual and encompasses the organization and the outside world as well.

- **Act decisively**

  o Communicate your support for your company's vision.

  o Develop your 360 visioning.

    ▪ Look within you to understand your dreams, strengths and weakness.

    ▪ Look behind you to appreciate your competence and experience. They have taught to be the person you are now.

    ▪ Look outside to the world for inspiration and understanding. Your leadership ultimately will be for the outside world.

    ▪ Look ahead towards the future. Leadership is essentially a future-looking exercise.

    ▪ Look up to the mentors, leaders and inspiring people above you. Look up to them for guidance and inspiration

    ▪ Look down towards the people you lead. They are the only reason you are a leader. Understand what they want out of you.

STEP 3: RACE TOWARDS DISRUPTION

- **Impact change**

  o You will have a better understanding of the global industry scenario and the changing landscape.

o   You will be able to anticipate the changes towards disruption faster and better. You will be highly valued for your leadership insights.

- **Take charge**

    o   Forecast how do you foresee changes in the market and how do you defend yourselves from the attacks out of the blue.

    o   Reflect on how you can lead your people and your company when the changes are so unpredictable and fast.

    o   As a leader analyse how do you predict the distance between the noose on your work and your strategy or product.

    o   Analyse the anatomy of uncertainty in your industry. In your organization

    o   Anticipate the changes of disruption by looking at the triggers.

    o   Identify specific skills and work styles that will fit in your future plan and current team structure, and recruit accordingly.

- **Act decisively**

    o   Look at trends

    o   Look at scalability

    o   Take the responsibility to explore new areas of interest, and seek adequate training to develop yourself for new responsibilities.

    o   Read the latest industry trend journals, magazines, and newsletters to keep current on new industry developments, your competition's advancement, and disruptive changes in the industry.

    o   Join networks and trade associations and become involved in their network. The network will help your net worth.

STEP 4: OWN YOUR FOLLOWERS

- **Impact change**

  o You will be able to create an inclusive culture and ensure productivity is maintained.

  o People's talents will be utilized fully and this will give a sense of being valued by the organization. This is an important step towards creating more leaders and a strong work culture.

- **Take charge**

  o Realize that your followers have changed their ways of working and preferences in leaders.

  o Explore the power of the changing ecosystem towards platform business ecosystem and evaluate your leadership skills to successfully lead such a system.

  o Realize that differences in age, culture and background are advantages, not deficits, for effective teamwork and problem-solving.

  o Create an inclusive work environment by utilizing the full potential of all employees and building on complementary skills, backgrounds, and cultural knowledge.

  o Assess the different learning styles and strengths in people you lead and understand that they have different views on how they want to be led.

  o Explore ways to use different generations of people and talents advantageously.

  o Recognize that cooperating and collaborating with others will enable you to achieve more than you could alone.

- **Act decisively**

  o Involve your team in your decision-making and problem-solving processes.

o   Build personal relationships with your team and truly understand them.

o   Encourage people to come up with different ideas and make them feel valued even if their ideas cannot be implemented.

o   Confront people who stereotype others and are unable to work towards inclusivity.

o   Set clear goals on feedbacks and ensure everyone analyses performances and never personalities.

o   Create events for intergenerational fun.

o   Conduct team-building sessions for your team.

STEP 5: KINDLE V.I.T.A.L CONVERSATIONS

- **Impact change**

o   To create a culture that builds execution muscles and also enriches relationships; one that embraces new ways is fiercely inclusive and yet when you walk into a room, a meeting, you feel it's your own corporate way.

o   As a conversational leader, you can connect, influence and inspire people around them one conversation at a time.

- **Take charge**

o   Strive to understand what motivates each of your employees through observation and dialogues. Don't make any assumptions.

o   Invite continuous feedback from your team.

o   Encourage the free flow of business, technical and informal information across the organization.

o   Evaluate the possible intentions and outcome of a conversation before you start talking.

o Encourage your partner to share their views and invite them to a conversation.

o Listen and recognize the perspective of your people always and gain ideas and trust.

o Look for trust and engagement in all conversations and suspend judgement while you listen.

o Foster an environment based on the clarity of communication, feedback on performance and the shared belief of belonging.

o Create networks of relationships that get work done

o Frequently press your confidence in your team and support them with what they do.

- **Act decisively**

o Have more one-on-one meetings to establish rapport and to learn others' viewpoints.

o When you are questioned, respond in a non-defensive manner; this gives people permission to question and creates a more open and honest mode of communication.

o Ask powerful questions in every conversation

o Include time for listening in your everyday schedule.

o Communicate persuasively so that people will understand and have clarity on what you want to convey.

STEP 6: EMPOWER YOUR ENTREPRENEURS

- **Impact change**

o Empowering builds confidence in your team to execute your shared vision establishes trust and builds the secondary level of leadership required to run the organization.

- **Take charge**

  o Build trust to foster collaboration. Work on your competence, commitment and connection with people.

  o Share your vision and your glory. Make your people strive for the moon and feel the pride of having done so.

  o Boundary the vision but unleash individual roles to achieve them.

  o Boundary the process but unleash employee way of working and dynamic problem-solving.

  o Boundary the values that the organization has but unleash how your employees show this value to their team and customers.

  o Do not allow your fears to dictate your leadership.

  o Connect people to opportunities and empower them to take decisions.

  o Build leadership in others, throughout the organization.

- **Act decisively**

  o Do not micromanage. Discourage the acts of micromanaging in your team members.

  o Learn to delegate effectively. Delegate assignments and let go! Empower people to pursue the assignment their way, within set parameters and deadlines.

  o Do not worry about losing control. You can influence people better by allowing them to grow. You can never control another human being. Control is a feeling born out of fear and exists only in your mind.

  o Clearly communicate how others' goals are compatible with your goals and how their success benefits you.

  o Show your trust in others first. Create an environment of trust and faith.

STEP 7: SCALE THE MOMENT

- **Impact change**
  - o You convey your leadership through your actions, commentary and behaviour. These are your leadership moments. Scale every one of these moments to build trust and inspiration in your people.

- **Take charge**
  - o Be a role model. Demonstrate and express your belief that you and your business partners will share leadership, take ownership for your work, and collaborate with each other as a team.

  - o Create a rhythm out of the various divergent people, pattern groups and interests and integrate them in time.

  - o Align the dynamics among the leader, the follower and the issue at hand or the moment where the leadership is required.

  - o Transform stressful and stretched experiences into learning opportunities.

  - o Open your mind and eyes to experience the leadership moments in others and learn from their moment of greatness or failure.

- **Act decisively**
  - o Understand what is required out of you as a leader at that dynamic moment in time. What leadership style, knowledge, skill is demanded from you by the moment.

  - o Accept experiences and moments that stretch your capabilities. Test yourself continuously and learn from the experience.

  - o Conduct after-action reviews of your leadership and ask for feedback and solicit mentoring wherever required.

The real test in leadership is in the action and walking the principles. Use this book to cover your base. As mentioned earlier, if leadership is a journey, this book is your GPS. The seven steps towards leading in uncertain times will guide you towards success.

ABOUT THE AUTHOR

Dr Latha Vijaybaskar catalyses positive transformations. She coaches teams and individuals to lead, engage and inspire action. As the founder and CEO of V.I.T.A.L Conversations, Latha is on a mission to enhance productive engagement and positive leadership.

Working with Latha, people discover the power of positive and appreciative conversation

- Right from the inner monologues in self-leadership
- Everyday conversations that matter in building a dedicated team
- To high performance conversations in leadership

Latha has approximately 20 years of experience in training and teaching, working in the corporate, educational and social sectors. She has coached, trained and taught more than 2,000 millennial leaders to lead, engage and drive positive transformations.

Her approach is based on exhaustive research in positive psychology, organizational communication, millennial leadership, appreciative enquiry and coaching conversations. In her bestselling book, *21 Difficult Conversations: Tools to Navigate Your Most Important Talk and Master Exactly What to Say*, she has captured the collective queries of her participants.

Latha is a learner first. Her accumulated credentials include a PhD in management with her thesis on 'Positive Organizational Communication', an MBA, a master's degree in psychology and an MPhil in organizational communication, and being a certified coach.

Reach out at latha@drlathavijaybaskar.com to understand how you can make positive transformations.